SO-BHY-950

Pierre Elliott Trudeau's
Great Betrayal

Pierre Elliott Trudeau's Great Betrayal

1st Edition

Copyright ©2017 The Interim Publishing Company.
Published by
The Interim Publishing Company.

All rights reserved. No part of this publication may be reproduced, distributed, or transmitted in any form or by any means, including photocopying, recording, or other electronic or mechanical methods, without the prior written permission of the publisher, except in the case of brief quotations embodied in critical reviews and certain other noncommercial uses permitted by copyright law. For permission requests, write to the publisher at the address below.

The Interim Publishing Company
104 Bond St. Ste 300
Toronto, ON M5B 1X9

Printed in the United States of America

Book Design: David Bolton

ISBN 978-1-54299-918-2

Pierre Elliott Trudeau's Great Betrayal

By
C. Gwendolyn Landolt, LLB
&
Patrick Redmond, PhD

Contents

Dedication

═══

This book is dedicated to all those many individuals who, although their names may not be mentioned in this book, have made a major difference with their dedication and sacrifices on behalf of the child in the womb. Without them the pro-life movement could not have carried on over these years. Many of its successes have been due to them.

They have laboured in the vineyard in the heat of the noonday sun, with selfless determination because they could not turn away from the cries of the unborn child. Their faithfulness is the very foundation of and a monument to a future pro-life Canada.

Acknowledgements

We wish to acknowledge the immense contribution made to the study of abortion in Canada by Fr. Alphonse de Valk, CSB in his 1974 book entitled *Morality and Law in Canadian politics – The Abortion Controversy*. This book offers a clear and all-encompassing analysis of the legalization of abortion by Pierre Trudeau and the Liberals in their 1969 Omnibus Bill. We benefited from his valuable work and are indebted to him for it.

Also, mention must be made of Jim Hughes, who became involved in the great struggle against abortion in the late 1970s and who has continued, to this day, to lead the fight in Canada for justice for the unborn and newly born. His leadership in the efforts of Campaign Life has been invaluable. Jim made available the extensive archives of Campaign Life to the authors. For this we are deeply grateful.

Finally, we wish to extend our deepest thanks to Dan Di Rocco, Mary Ellen Douglas, Pat Loughran and Suzanne Marson who reviewed the text and offered many corrections and valuable improvements. Finally, many thanks to Helen Caruso for her endless patience in preparing this manuscript.

Preface

The reader may, at times, be confused with the dates in the book. In one chapter, there may be references to the 1970s then the 1980s. Then in the next chapter the story returns to the 1970s. The reason for this is that we covered the legalization of abortion from the viewpoint of the major players in the process, including Trudeau and the Liberal party, the Progressive Conservative Party, the judges, the Catholic Church and the pro-life movement. These have separate chapters. To improve the flow within each chapter, the reader sometimes goes back and forth in time. We trust this will prove acceptable.

Introduction

In Canada, abortion, at any time during a pregnancy was made a felony in 1841. The legal prohibition of abortion was included in the Canadian Criminal Code when it was passed in 1892. There were several slight rewordings of the code provisions prohibiting abortion in 1906, 1927 and again in 1954.

However, from 1969 to 1982, dramatic changes took place. A great betrayal of the Christian principles upon which Canada was founded took place. The Liberals, under Prime Minister Pierre Trudeau, passed an Omnibus Bill in 1969 legalizing abortion under certain conditions. Again under Trudeau, another negative milestone was reached when the Liberal government passed the Charter of Rights in 1982. This constitutional change led to the Supreme Court of Canada removing all protection from the unborn and allowed abortion on demand, up to, during, and after the birth of the child.

This study is about those who knew what was happening and who fought to stop it.

Chapter 1

A changing society 1950s-1960s

M any changes were taking place in Canada during the 1950s and 1960s that promoted a more secular society, where fewer and fewer restraints would be placed on individual actions.

Moral values, in particular, were changing dramatically.

With the development of the contraceptive pill, women gained a new control over their fertility, deciding when and with whom they might want to conceive, if at all. The pill increased sexual activity. When the pill failed, there was abortion. So the demand for abortion increased.

Sexual liberation led women to have more independence and freedom than previously. Women's liberation produced radical feminism.

With women freed from child-bearing, the institution of marriage itself began to be redefined. If children were not necessary, then neither was marriage. With the introduction of no-fault divorce, the rate of divorce rose quickly and the demands and responsibilities of marriage were becoming less desirable.

The introduction of a "sex without consequences" mentality and intercourse divorced from reproduction inevitably encouraged a change in other social attitudes. As sexual freedom extended

1

throughout society, a previously quiet homosexual movement became more open and started making demands on society.

The influence of Great Britain

In his landmark study on the legalization of abortion with the Omnibus Bill of 1969, historian Fr. Alphonse de Valk wrote in detail on the powerful influence that laws and practices in Great Britain had on legislators in Canada. This section is based on his analysis. [1]

Fr. de Valk stated that:

"The Canadian movement to widen the grounds for abortion had its primary ideological origins in Great Britain."

Two reasons were given for this. One was the fact that English Canada often reflected the British moral values. The second was that British political parties were parent to the ideology of Canadian parties.

A seminal report written in 1957 by Sir John Wolfenden also laid the foundation for a new interpretation of the role of morality in the exercise of law. Wolfenden's report, called the *Report of the Committee on Homosexual Offenses and Prostitution* was to have a critical effect on the future abortion controversy in that it laid down principles that would later be applied to abortion and other moral issues. In answering the question as to what acts should be punished by the state, it noted that the function of criminal law:

> *"is to preserve public order and decency, to protect the citizen from what is offensive or injurious, and to provide safeguards against exploitation and corruption of others, particularly those who are specially vulnerable because they are young, weak in body or mind, inexperienced, or in a state of special physical, official or economic dependence...*
>
> *There must remain a realm of private morality and immorality which is ... not the law's business."*

In 1967, under a Labour government in the UK, a reformed abortion law was passed, making abortion legal and justifiable in four categories:

> *"- where there is 'serious risk to the life or grave injury to the health, whether physical or mental' of the pregnant woman,*

'before at or after the birth of a child'.

-where 'there is a substantial risk that if the child were born it would suffer from such physical or mental abnormalities as to be seriously handicapped'.

-where 'the pregnant woman's capacity as a mother' would be 'severely overstrained by the care of the child or of another child as the case may be'.

-where the woman becomes pregnant while 'under the age of sixteen' or as the result of rape."

Canada would soon adopt much of this reformed abortion law.

Changes in the United States

Fr. de Valk also noted changes happening in the United States that would influence Canada.[2] Individuals and groups began advocating a more liberal approach to abortion from the 1950s onwards. In 1959 the American Law Institute proposed a radical liberalizing of abortions in its first presentation of a reform of criminal law, called the Model Penal Code. By the 1960s those promoting abortion demanded greater liberalization. Also during that decade, more and more media pushed for liberalized abortion laws. These pressures and influences resulted in the legalization of abortions in many jurisdictions.

By 1970, 14 American states had changed their abortion laws, including New York, which had removed practically all restrictions.

The promotion of abortion in Canada

Abortion was being recommended in Canada as well since the late 1950s. Leading the push was the woman's magazine *Chatelaine* under the feminist editor Doris Anderson. Other magazines then took up the cause. They were followed by media especially *The Globe and Mail*, which had started promoting abortion by 1961. Then the United Church followed in its own magazine, the United Church *Observer*. At its 19th General Council in 1960, the United Church had already approved the legality of therapeutic abortions for physical or mental reasons. The Rev. Ray Goodall wrote in 1963:

> *"that the Canadian abortion law was not only wrong but cruel and 'grossly immoral'." (3)*

3

The Globe and Mail noted on January 2, 1963:

> *"Pressure for the reform of the laws governing abortion has been growing in recent years at many levels of Canadian society. Highly placed members of the legal, medical and university professions have urged the extension of legal abortion. The National Council of Women presented a brief to the Royal Commission on Health Services which disclosed that illegal abortion is the commonest cause of maternal mortality in Canada. Leading clergymen of major Protestant communions and of the Jewish faith endorsed extension of legal abortion. Members of Parliament representing all four political parties had also gone on record as favouring extension."*

After this article was published, the legal and medical professions also came out in favour of abortion.

Members of the Canadian Bar Association proposed a motion to legalize abortion at their annual meeting in Banff in 1963. The resolution was sponsored by the British Columbia Subsection on Criminal Justice under the chairmanship of A. Stewart Mc-Morran. This was strongly opposed by the B.C. Catholic Lawyers Guild. The motion was deferred. The motion was brought up again in 1964 and 1965 but deferred both times. At their 1966 meeting, the resolution was sent to all members. Those promoting legalization of abortion referenced the recent approving of abortion in the UK.

By 1966, Fr. de Valk writes:

> *"the climate of opinion among the population had shifted so much that approval of the resolution was a foregone conclusion."*

He noted that lawyers were split into two groups: those that wanted to address illegal abortions and those that wanted to address whether abortion was moral or immoral and whether it was good or bad for society. Stuart McMorran, then Chairman of the Criminal Justice section, once again introduced the resolution to legalize abortion.

Fr. de Valk writes that except for a passing reference by one doctor, not one of those who favoured legalizing abortion or widening the grounds for abortion seemed interested in discussing the issue of human life.

Some lawyers opposed legalization. Alex Saranchuk, Crown prosecutor in Winnipeg, stated:

> "Life was bestowed by God not by man; that one could not justify destruction of innocent human life; that everyone agreed that the child is human just before birth; that since it is impossible to demonstrate the precise time when the unborn becomes human, it leaves the moment of conception as the only rational choice; that except for emergencies to save the mother's life, churches such as the United Church and the Anglican Church had opposed abortion as recently as 1960 and 1958; that there was much dispute whether or not therapeutic abortions were good medicine; that medical indications for therapeutic abortions were minimal; that some psychiatrists held that there were no real psychiatric grounds for termination of pregnancy either; and that in the early months of pregnancy doctors could not state whether a child would be born defective." [4]

Another who spoke against abortion was Sydney Paikin who stressed the rights of the unborn child, quoting the United Nations 1959 Declaration on Human Rights:

> "The child by reason of its physical and mental immaturity needs special safeguards and care, including appropriate legal protection before as well as after birth." [5]

Yet the majority opinion in the Canadian Bar Association was in favour of abortion and of dismissing religious and moral objections. So the vote in favour of abortion carried.

The Canadian Medical Association also began to promote the legalization of abortion. Raised first in 1961 by British Columbia doctors, it was then strongly promoted by doctors in Ontario. The Sterilization and Therapeutic Abortion Committee reported to the Council of the Ontario Medical Association in May 1965 recommending that:

> "operations terminating a pregnancy be lawful if performed 'to preserve the life or physical or the mental health" of the mother, and if they were done in a properly qualified place and manner, after consultation with an abortion committee".

The Council of the Ontario Medical Association approved the recommendations. It then went to the Committee on Maternal Welfare of the Canadian Medical Association and was approved with minor modifications.

In June 1967, the general council of the Canadian Medical Association adopted deformity and sexual offences as grounds for terminating a pregnancy. Some doctors opposed this, including Dr. Tallon of Cornwall.

Gerald Waring, in his article in the *C.M.A.J.* November 1967, offered some insight into the motivations of those promoting abortion. He identified the doctors promoting abortion at the hearings of the Commons committee considering legislation to legalize abortion as including Dr. Aitken, the Assistant Secretary of the CMA, Dr. Gregg Tompkins of Halifax, and Drs. Douglas Cannell and Donald Low of Toronto, and Dr. Kenneth Gray. He quoted Dr. Lewis Brand (PC, Saskatoon) who referred to them as distinguished lawbreakers and Robert Stanbury (L, York-Scarborough) who noted them as "the biggest gathering of criminal abortionists ever held in Canada".[6]

Fr. de Valk noted that the general public became more supportive of the option of abortion after 1965, when the thalidomide pill, given to pregnant women, led to the birth of deformed babies in Canada and elsewhere.

The United Church of Canada, at the 22nd annual meeting of the General Council in September 1966 adopted a resolution justifying abortion "when the life of the foetus threatens the life or health of the mother."

Some national organizations started supporting abortion. The Central Ontario Women's Institute, in 1965, called abortion laws "archaic and futile". The National Council of Women of Canada adopted a resolution in June 1964 at its annual meeting in favour of legal abortions. It presented the resolutions to the government in 1965 and 1966. As Fr. de Valk writes:

> *"It urged the Government to establish a Royal Commission to provide 'an objective and non-partisan basis for amending the law,' it also called the existing law 'confused, conflicting, outdated, and in certain instances, cruel and unjust', thus leaving no doubt about its own attitude. The reason*

given for this resolution was the need 'to bring these laws into conformity with the realities of Canadian life'." [7]

A few organizations spoke out against abortion. The Catholic Women's League at its 46th national convention in Hamilton in September 1966 urged the government to reject broader abortion laws.

Changes in the Catholic Church

The Catholic Church in Canada, for many decades, had been influential in the development of government policies. This was due, in no little part, to the fact that 46% of the population of Canada was Roman Catholic and the Liberal party up to and including 1980-1, when the Charter was being negotiated, consisted primarily of Catholics.[8]

In the 1960s and 1970s, a number of changes took place in the Roman Catholic Church which influenced its relations with the government, its own position in Canadian society, in the country and its public policies.

One of the major factors causing this change was the Second Vatican Council of 1962-1965. In a number of its documents, it modified significantly the relationship between the Catholic Church and the state.[9]

For example, Pope Paul VI, in the Vatican Council II document, *Dignitatis humanae # 2*, proclaimed the right to religious freedom. He stated:

> *"This Vatican synod declares that the human person has a right to religious freedom. Such freedom consists in this, that all should have such immunity from coercion by individuals, or by groups, or by any human power, that no one should be forced to act against his conscience in religious matters, nor prevented from acting according to his conscience, whether in private or in public, within due limits... This right of the human person to religious freedom should have such recognition in the regulation of society as to become a civil right."*

Until that statement, the Church had taught the opposite, that religious freedom should be curtailed for the sake of truth and to prevent the spread of heresies and false philosophies that harmed civil societies.

In 1864, in *Quanta Cura*, #3, Pope Pius IX condemned the idea that every man should be granted the civil right to religious belief, writing:

> *"From which totally false idea of social government they do not fear to foster that erroneous opinion, most fatal in its effects on the Catholic Church and the salvation of souls, called by our predecessor, Gregory XVI, an insanity, namely, that 'liberty of conscience' and worship is each man's personal right, which ought to be legally proclaimed and asserted in every rightly constituted society."*

Pope Leo XIII, *Libertas* (# 21-23), June 20, 1888 reinforced this thinking:

> *"Justice therefore forbids, and reason itself forbids, the State to be godless; or to adopt a line of action which would end in godlessness – namely, to treat the various religions (as they call them) alike, and to bestow upon them promiscuously equal rights and privileges. Since, then, the profession of one religion is necessary in the State, that religion must be professed which alone is true, and which can be recognized without difficulty, especially in the Catholic States, because the marks of truth are, as it were, engraven upon it... Men have a right freely and prudently to propagate throughout the State what things soever are true and honorable, so that as many as possible may possess them; but lying opinions, than which no mental plague is greater, and vices which corrupt the heart and moral life should be diligently repressed by public authority, lest they insidiously work the ruin of the State."*

Pope Benedict XVI, while a Cardinal, acknowledged this dramatic change, and supported it, writing in 1982 in *Principles of Catholic Theology*:

> *"If it is desirable to offer a diagnosis of the text [of the Vatican II document, Gaudium et Spes] as a whole, we might say that (in conjunction with the texts on religious liberty and world religions) it is a revision of the Syllabus of Pius IX, a kind of counter syllabus... As a result, the one-sidedness of the position adopted by the Church under Pius IX and Pius X in response to the situation created by the new phase of*

history inaugurated by the French Revolution was, to a large extent, corrected."

He later modified this thinking and, in an interview with *Avvenire* on March 16, 2016, reflected on how belief in salvation outside the church has undermined the foundation of the faith.

As a result of the promotion of religious liberty by the Second Vatican II Council, a number of Catholic nations amended their constitutions to become secular nations. For example, the constitutions of Catholic Spain and Colombia were actually changed at the express direction of the Vatican, to permit the public practice of non-Catholic religions.

Thus in Spain, the *"Ley Organica del Estado"*, of January 10, 1967, replaced the second paragraph of article 6 with the following:

"The State will assume the protection of religious liberty which will be under the protection of the Judiciary responsible for safeguarding morals and public order."

Spain went from being a Catholic nation to being a "godless one", which now gave legal protection to divorce, sodomy, pornography and contraception.

The changes being implemented in Spain were taking place in the province of Quebec as well. Cardinal Léger, the Archbishop of Montreal, was a member of the Central Preparatory Commission for Vatican II. He had close ties with fellow cardinals who were at the forefront of renewal: Franz König of Vienna, Julius August Döpfner of Munich, Josef Frings of Cologne, Achille Liénart of Lille, Bernard Jan Alfrink of Utrecht, Leo Jozef Suenens of Mechelen-Brussels, Giovanni Battista Montini, later Pope Paul VI, of Milan, and Augustin Bea, President of the Pontifical Council.

Cardinal Léger pressed for modernization and renewal in the church. Among the ideas he promoted were: ecumenism; the family and the underlying topics of procreation and marriage; freedom of thought within the church and religious freedom. He asked that the question of contraception be left open.

With Archbishop Roy of Quebec City and the other bishops of the province of Quebec, he engaged in delicate negotiations with the provincial government of Jean Lesage, which resulted in major institutional restructuring in the fields of health, social services, and education, particularly with regard to *Bill 60*, which led to the creation of a Department of Education in 1964. These negotiations greatly diminished the role of the Catholic Church in much of life in "la belle province".

Cardinal Léger, working with the priests in his archdiocese at putting *aggiornamento* into practice was not easy, and his relations with his fellow bishops were difficult. While the church grew in numbers, it lost many priests after 1966. When he resigned in 1968, the church had changed greatly in Quebec.

The hierarchy of the church in Quebec would be one of the regional associations of bishops that were most supportive of many of the changes proposed in the Charter of Rights, particularly the section on bilingualism. (10)

Vatican II also changed ideas on contraception. The Vatican II document *Gaudium et Spes* # 51 stated:

> *"Those who are learned in the sciences, especially in the biological, medical, social and psychological fields, can be of considerable service to the good of marriage and the family, and to the peace of conscience, if they collaborate in trying to throw more light on the various conditions which favor the virtuous control of procreation."*

At # 87:

> *"For, according to the inalienable human right to marriage and parenthood, the decision about the number of children to have, lies with the right judgment of the parents, and cannot in any way be entrusted to the judgment of public authority... In exploring methods to help couples regulate the number of their children, appropriate information should be given on scientific advances that are well proven and are found to be in accordance with the moral order."*

The Disaster of the Winnipeg Statement in 1968

The openness to change led many Canadian members of the hierarchy of bishops, at their conference in Winnipeg in 1968, advised by theologians and others, to reject Pope Paul's encyclical *Humanae Vitae*, when it condemned the use of contraceptives, and to issue their own *Winnipeg Statement* allowing it. Paragraph 26 was the key paragraph:

"26. Counselors may meet others who, accepting the teaching of the Holy Father, find that because of particular circumstances they are involved in what seems to them a clear conflict of duties, e.g. the reconciling of conjugal love and responsible parenthood with the education of children already born or with the health of the mother. In accord with the accepted principles of moral theology, if these persons have tried sincerely but without success to pursue a line of conduct in keeping with the given directives, they may be safely assured that whoever honestly chooses that course which seems right to him does so in good conscience." [11]

The rejection of spiritual leadership from Rome by the Canadian Bishops constituted a decisive break with the teaching of the Universal Church, and set up something like a Church of Canada. Cardinal Edouard Gagnon, P.S.S. said that the Bishops who supported the *Winnipeg Statement* were in schism. Monsignor Vincent Foy, a cannon lawyer, in an article published in *Catholic Insight*, October 2003, stated:

"In truth, because of that statement, the Church in Canada is now stricken and dying. There is no hope for a viable and evangelizing Church here until the teaching of that Statement is cancelled and replaced with the truth."

He then gave fifty reasons why the Winnipeg Statement was so wrong. These reasons included the following:

1. *"The Winnipeg Statement is tantamount to blasphemy. It is God who determines what is morally good and evil.*
2. *It is contrary to the first commandment of God. In following the Winnipeg Statement, one's mind stops being in conformity with God's.*
3. *It substitutes the authority of man for the authority of Christ.*
4. *It has increased tolerance for dissent.*
5. *It advocates relativism or situation ethics.*
6. *It teaches an erroneous doctrine on conscience, teaching that one may form one's conscience in opposition to God's law.*
7. *It was an act of disobedience to the Holy See.*
8. *As a result of its permissiveness, many theologians and*

others have felt free to dissent from Church teachings on issues such as homosexuality, the ordination of women and abortion.

9. *It was the seed bed to new and disastrous sex education.*

10. *It has lowered the level of ethics among Catholic politicians, judges, lawyers, doctors, pharmacists, nurses, hospital staff, teachers and catechists.*

11. *It made it difficult to discipline nominal Catholics like Pierre Trudeau, John Turner and Jean Chrétien who have been principally responsible for the chasm between Church and State in the area of divine moral law."*

In another article, published in *Catholic Insight* in October 2010, entitled *Recovering Humanae Vitae in Canada*, Msgr. Foy noted:

"By the Winnipeg Statement, Canadian bishops became promoters of mass murder and complicit in turning thousands of sewers into tombs."

He considered the fruits of this break with the universal church to be:

"Adultery, fornication, venereal disease, pornography, radical feminism, sterilization, violence, child abuse, corrupt family life education, abortion and euthanasia".[12]

In 2008 the Canadian bishops issued a Pastoral Letter called *Liberating Potential*. In it, all the faithful were invited to discover or rediscover the encyclical *Humanae Vitae*. This attempt at retraction has been ignored by most Catholics.

Thus, Vatican II and the changes it proposed advanced by the Canadian Catholic hierarchy at Winnipeg weakened the Canadian church in resistance to a powerful secular tide being advanced by Pierre Trudeau and the Liberal party, as we shall see.

To sum up, the Catholic Church in Canada, rather than being the protector and guarantor of the received wisdom and teaching of the ages was instead prepared to collaborate with "modernizing" forces that were gathering momentum.

Chapter 2

Trudeau legalizes abortion in 1969

Trudeau's Background

While studying at Brébeuf College, in Montreal, Trudeau had met Marie-Joseph d'Anjou and Rodolphe Dubé. Father Dubé was renowned not only for his teaching but also for his writings, published under his nom de plume, François Hertel. He became influential in debates about faith, politics, and Quebec's destiny, especially among the young. Charismatic, brilliant, and often outrageous, Hertel increasingly drew Pierre and his brother Charles into his circle. In the case of Pierre, he became a confidant. An advocate of personalism, Hertel encouraged Trudeau to read philosophers Jacques Maritain and Emmanuel Mounier. The devout but rebellious young Catholic found their approach to personal liberty emancipating, although he also found corporatist thought and the conservative nationalism of Charles Maurras compelling.[1]

Personalism has many interpretations, but for Trudeau it meant that:

> "The person ... is the individual enriched with a social conscience, integrated into the life of the communities around him and the economic context of his time, both of which

must in turn give persons the means to exercise their freedom of choice."[2]

Allen Mills, a professor of political science at the University of Winnipeg, and author of a recent intellectual biography of Trudeau, writes that Trudeau's personalism held that a liberal order rested upon respect for the conscience of each citizen.[3]

Refined by later studies, this personalism formed the core of Trudeau's religious understanding of the relationship between the individual and society. The rights of the individual over the group would become an important component of the Charter of Rights.

Hertel influenced Trudeau's radicalism. Trudeau participated in the Frères-Chasseurs, who planned to rise up against the "oppressors in Ottawa". He took part in street riots, and worked in a secret society, the LX, to overthrow what they considered a corrupt system. He became involved in the Bloc Populaire Canadien, which had taken the lead in the anti-conscription campaign of the early 1940s. Father d'Anjou pressed him to take on the editorship of a nationalist journal promoting the notion of *Laurentia,* a French-speaking autonomous state. He met several times with l'Abbé Lionel Groulx, a noted French-Canadian nationalist who supported French Marshal Philippe Pétain's government at Vichy, and supported nationalist causes.

In 1944 Trudeau went to Harvard University. There he was influenced by the numerous European exiles, many of them Jewish, who taught him, notably Wassily W. Leontief, Joseph Alois Schumpeter, Carl Joachim Friedrich, and Gottfried Haberler. He heard about John Maynard Keynes for the first time. He was also intrigued by liberal and democratic traditions and the separation of the spiritual from the secular in public life.

In 1946 he decided to continue his studies in France, where he audited courses at the *Institut d'Études Politiques de Paris.* His major interest in Paris was the stirring debates among French post-war intellectuals, particularly among Catholics. Like Trudeau, Emmanuel Mounier was discarding corporatist, collectivist, and elitist aspects of pre-war personalism and shaping the doctrine for the post-war era. Trudeau enthusiastically attended lectures and meetings with Mounier and other Catholic intellectuals such as the Jesuit, Pierre Teilhard de Chardin, and Étienne Gilson. In a nation where communism thrived, Mounier's attempt to find a balance between Soviet communism and Christianity impressed Trudeau.

Significantly, in his last key editorial before his death, Mounier wrote in his journal *Esprit,* the proletariat:

> *"...must be allowed to continue the positive work of the communist party while eliminating all the poisons which are mixed therein. Such is one of our principal tasks for tomorrow. We will emphasize that as much as possible in our review, and our wish is that one day we can work together in such a task with a purified communism."* [4]

From Paris Trudeau went to England in the fall of 1947 to study at the London School of Economics and Political Science. He quickly found that the eminent Labour Party intellectual, Harold Joseph Laski, shared his belief in the need for reconciliation between the West and Soviet communism and his doubts about the fervent anti-communism of Britain's Labour government. Laski and the London School of Economics had a greater intellectual influence on him than his experiences in Paris, particularly in spurring his understanding of democratic socialism.

Trudeau stated that he found Professor Harold Laski of the London School of Economics (LSE) "the most stimulating and powerful influence" he had encountered. In Laski's single most important book, *A Grammar of Politics* which Trudeau studied while at LSE, Laski wrote "There cannot, in a word, be democracy, unless there is socialism".

Trudeau also learned the philosophy of T.H. Green whose liberalism stated:

> *"The focal point was not the state but the individual – the individual seen as a person integrated into society, which is to say endowed with fundamental rights and essential liberties, but also with responsibilities."* [5]

Students with him at LSE, a hotbed of socialist thinking, noted that Trudeau went much further with his "flirtations with Marxism". Trudeau's fascination with socialism also permeated his uncompleted doctoral thesis where he explored the interplay between Christianity and Marxism. [6]

To Trudeau, the world was evolving toward socialism and more:

"The party of the people – socialism, communism – will eventually come out the winner". [7]

He also watched the welfare society being developed by the Labour party.

He also grew less enamored with nationalism. He felt the world was moving into a post-nationalist age, which ideally:

"will be one in which citizens will increasingly see themselves as conscience-driven persons moving in a world of great diversity and opportunity and living the life of democratic participation and universal freedom. Each person will be constrained less and less by group affiliation and will be shaped more and more by individual judgments and commitments that will constitute the person's network of relationships and the informal dialogical communities of the moment he moves in and out of. The freedom of the person to live according to conscience means that the identity of the individual will be one that is chosen and periodically revised and altered. There will be no presumption of superiority of communitarian identities but rather a series of encounters with the Other from which the person will derive opportunity for moral exploration, personal affirmation, and cultural development. The social world envisioned by Trudeau will be international as well as local." [8]

In 1949 Trudeau became a civil servant in the Privy Council in Ottawa. He liked the job, he said:

"Because as the secretariat to the Cabinet, it was the key decision-making centre, and because I wanted to observe in practice what I had just finished studying in theory." [9]

Trudeau enters politics

Trudeau dabbled with different political parties, including the Liberal party under Jean Lesage, because of the latter's determination to secularize Quebec society. He became disillusioned with Quebec nationalism and separatism, however, and attacked both in the journal, *Cité Libre*.

The decisive moment for Trudeau to enter politics occurred when he and Gérard Pelletier, a journalist with the daily newspaper *Le*

Devoir, went to the Eastern Townships to join striking asbestos workers. There, Trudeau and Pelletier, who had often met with Trudeau in Paris, sided with Jean Marchand, General Secretary of the Canadian Catholic Confederation of Labour, to press the cause of the strikers. The ruling Union Nationale government under Maurice Duplessis had reacted harshly to what it considered to be an illegal strike. The Catholic clergy was divided on the issue. The strike profoundly affected Trudeau, as he linked the evidence of working class action with his past studies of socialism, labour, and democracy.

On 10 Sept. 1965, Marchand, Pelletier, and Trudeau announced that they would be Liberal candidates in the next federal election.

Trudeau and Pelletier explained their decision in an article published on October 12, 1965 in *Cité Libre* and *Le Devoir*. They stated:

> *"It must never be forgotten that in the democracies that we know, the political party isn't an end but a means, not a goal, but an instrument. He who enters a political party, then, is choosing a tool.*
>
> *In the present case, the undersigned are still following the same goals, they are continuing to adhere to the same political ideologies that they have for a long time set forth in Cité Libre: a constitutionalism respectful of the rights of groups and individuals, a democracy aligned with social progress, a federalism which knows how to reconcile a strong, central power with progressive and autonomous provinces, finally, politics open to the left.*
>
> *Nevertheless, in the pursuance of these goals, the authors have opted for a means – the federal Liberal Party – which has caused some surprise.*
>
> *For us, there hasn't been any rupture, we don't repudiate any of our convictions. We have only resolved to pursue elsewhere and in other ways, the intellectual and social struggle which has always claimed us."*

After winning his seat in the Montreal riding of Mount Royal, in the 1965 federal election, Trudeau was appointed the Parliamentary Secretary for Prime Minister Lester Pearson. Trudeau found others in Ottawa who shared his concern that the government policy towards Quebec was one of drift. He met regularly with Marc

Lalonde, who had been appointed in 1967 to a full time position in the Privy Council Office as a special advisor on constitutional matters by Prime Minister Pearson. Lalonde was subsequently elected as the Liberal MP for the Montreal riding of Outremont and became the Minister of Health and Justice in Trudeau's Cabinet. Public servants such as Peter Michael Pitfield and Allan Ezra Gotlieb were also part of this group. Together, they began to craft a more coherent response to Quebec's constitutional challenges; one that rejected what they perceived as the weakness embodied in the cooperative federalism of the first Pearson years.

In March 1966, Trudeau and Marchand gained control of the Quebec wing of the federal Liberal Party, which had established its own administration. At its first meeting, the Quebec section supported motions drafted by Trudeau condemning "special status" or "a confederation of ten states" and approved the concept of a "bill of rights" within a constitution.

Liberals challenge existing moral laws

The Liberal government that Trudeau joined was already addressing a number of moral issues. Pressure from the Canadian Bar Association, the Canadian Medical Association, Protestant churches, media and various organizations were making them respond to demands for revisions in the Criminal Code on issues such as marriage, contraception, abortion and other moral issues.

The House set up a Standing Committee on Health and Welfare in 1966 to deal initially with contraception, then with abortion. They considered private bills which, if accepted, would bring changes to Section 150 of the Criminal Code, which discusses sexual offences against a minor. [10]

In addressing contraception, members of the committee wanted to remove contraception entirely from the Criminal Code. One member, Jean Paul Matte (L, Champlain) informed the committee that two priest professors, Fr. Louis P. Vezina, OMI superior of the Oblate Fathers' Centre for Ecclesiastical Studies in Ottawa, and Jean Guy Lemarier, OMI, moral theologian, explained that in their view Catholics would not be morally wrong if they favoured proposed changes in the Criminal Code. [11]

Support for legalization of contraception then came from the

Catholic Bishops of Canada who submitted a brief in October 1966 to the committee in which they stated:

> *"They would not oppose changes in the legislation on contraceptives if 'safeguards against irresponsible sales and advertising...were provided' and if personal freedom was protected."* [12]

The committee on Health and Welfare sent its final report to the Commons on December 5, 1966. It recommended that birth control be removed from the Criminal Code.

The Special Joint Committee of the Commons and Senate on Divorce, announced on March 15, 1966, began its hearings in the fall of 1966. Nine private bills were referred to it. Until then, the sole ground for divorce was adultery. These bills proposed adding many other justifications.

Of the Catholic Bishops' brief submitted in April, 1967, historian Fr. de Valk writes:

> *"While leaving the 'details about grounds for divorce that would be acceptable or not' to the 'well-informed conscience' of legislators, they stated that 'we cannot overemphasize that an indiscriminate broadening of the grounds for divorce is not the solution to the problem of unhappy marriages.' Instead they suggested an extensive rethinking of the entire body of legislation dealing with marriage and the family as a part of a revision of the divorce law, including important changes in the procedures of divorce courts."* [13]

The Committee submitted its report and draft bill in June 1967.

Separating law from morality

Into this changing moral environment came the argument that law and morality should be separate. *The Globe and Mail* strongly pushed this. Fr de Valk writes:

> *"By the close of 1966 the paper had repeatedly asserted that abortion was a question of private morality and that law, therefore, should not be concerned with it. As an explanation as to why the law had made abortion its concern in the past, the paper had offered religious beliefs, which it now declared to be both outmoded and representative only of a minority."* [14]

Trudeau becomes Justice Minister

On April 4, 1967 Pearson appointed Trudeau Minister of Justice and Attorney General. Trudeau quickly started implementing some of the radical changes that, ultimately, were to transform Canada.

Shortly after being appointed to the cabinet, Trudeau told journalist Peter Newman that:

> *"It was his intention to use his position as Justice Minister to advance societal change. Trudeau wanted to use his perch to plan for the society of tomorrow. Trudeau said he would apply the disciplines of sociology and economics to 'provide a framework for our evolving way of life... so there's no curtailment of intellectual or physical liberty'."* [15]

He concentrated primarily on the constitution and the much-delayed reform of the Criminal Code. The 47-year-old bachelor announced his plan to decriminalize homosexual acts between consenting adults, allow for easier divorces, and permit abortion if the mother's health was endangered.

Trudeau suggested that the public servants advising him were a radical force behind him. He wrote that they said:

> *"Of course, there's also the Criminal Code that needs to be brought up to date on a lot of sensitive and controversial issues such as homosexuality, firearms, abortion: there is also the divorce law, which is archaic...We need hardly tell you that several of these questions are quite delicate and politically dangerous. You know that as well as we do."*

He however decided:

> *"No, I prefer to start with the most difficult one. Let's go with the Criminal Code and the divorce law."* [16]

Bishops oppose changes to the abortion law

After Trudeau announced his intention to legalize many moral laws, the Catholic bishops responded, asking for a delay in any legislation. Fr. de Valk states:

> *"The Bishops were preparing a detailed report...In the meantime, the Church was giving up opposition to divorce reform on the same grounds that it had abandoned opposi-*

tion to the legalization of birth control. But the line was to be drawn at abortion, and the bishops did not like the government to include it in the same breath with divorce and birth control."[17]

After this was criticized by *The Globe and Mail*, Archbishop Philip Pocock of Toronto replied, stating that:

"The church might relax its opposition to proposed changes if research indicated change would be for the common good."[18]

Fr. de Valk lamented that the Bishops needed to be clear that their opposition was based on the defense of innocent human life and not on the common good, tied up with reducing illegal abortions or the number of abortions.[19]

In the continuing pressure by *The Globe and Mail* on the government to legalize abortions, it published a four part series by journalist Jean Howarth entitled "Abortion: A Matter of Conscience," starting May 25, 1967. Howarth demanded the right of women to decide their own destiny:

"The present law of Canada treats women where abortion is concerned ... as though their bodies were state property. If the rights of the individual were given absolute recognition, the decision of whether or not to have an abortion would reside wholly with the woman."

This demand became a rallying cry for feminists throughout the abortion debate.

Hearings of the Standing Committee on Health and Welfare

In October 1967, the Standing Committee on Health and Welfare started its hearings on abortion. It would continue until the beginning of March 1968. (20)

One of the MPs who had submitted a bill for consideration, H.W.Herridge (NDP, Kootenay West) claimed there were 100,000 to 300,000 illegal abortions in Canada. These ludicrous numbers were later rejected and denounced by pro-lifers and others. Another sponsor, Grace MacInnis (NDP, Vancouver-Kingsway) advocated legalizing abortion to produce 'a quality population.'

Some of the representatives on the committee spoke out strongly against revising the law. One of these was Ralph Cowan (L, York-

Humber) who rejected demands for 'a quality population' by asking if Queen Victoria should have been aborted because one arm was shorter than the other or if President Roosevelt should have been shot when he became paralyzed. Joseph O'Keefe (L, St John's East) said Hitler had already tried the 'quality population' line.

Among those who presented a brief was Dr. Henry Morgentaler, representing the Humanist Fellowships of Montreal, Toronto and Victoria. Stating that women had the inalienable right to mastery over their own bodies, he recommended abortion on demand for the first three months of pregnancy.[21]

Among the groups opposing abortion was the Emergency Organization for the Defense of Unborn Children, formed in Ottawa in September 1967 by Philip Cooper. This organization later became the Alliance for Life, run out of Ottawa. Then it transferred to Toronto and became the National Alliance for Life.

Philip Cooper spoke to the committee for his group. He noted:

"When we find ourselves killing off our unwanted babies, why not our old people, our crippled, our blind and our sick? Why not all inmates of prisons and mental institutions?"

When asked if he thought those then supporting abortion would do such a thing, he replied no, but added rather prophetically:

"We are laying the framework for other people who come after us ... when we blaze a trail, we do not know how far other people are going along that trail." [22]

Among others who spoke out against abortion were Dr. Paul Adams and Dr. Kevin Ford, representing the Catholic Physicians Guild of Manitoba, Dr. Tallon from Cornwall, Dr. F Clarke Fraser from Montreal and lawyer David Dehler from Ottawa.

The Canadian Conference of Catholic Bishops was scheduled to make a presentation before the committee but their meeting was cancelled and reset for a date in 1968.

In December 1967 the Committee submitted an Interim Report advising a revision of the law. This was a surprise to many on the Committee. Only 11 of the 24 members were present on December 19 when it was submitted, and of these 11 members, 9 voted for it, a far cry from a majority.

It recommended that the Criminal Code be amended to "allow

therapeutic abortion under appropriate medical safeguards where a pregnancy will seriously endanger the life or the health of the mother."[23]

Trudeau introduces Omnibus Bill to allow abortion

When the Interim Report was submitted in December 1967, Trudeau acted quickly to legalize abortion and change other moral laws. On Dec 21, two days after receiving the Interim Report of the Standing Committee on Health and Welfare, the Government deposited in the House of Commons a 72 page, 104 clause, Omnibus bill, which covered a great many revisions in the Criminal Code, including the legalization of abortion. That same day, within hours of adjournment for the Christmas holiday, the bill was given first reading by the Commons.[24]

The *Calgary Herald* reported on December 20, 1967 that Trudeau felt that:

> "...these amendments would have a better chance at passing if they were included in a bigger, diverse bill with its obvious advantages of psychological inertia".

Trudeau also informed reporters that he saw no reason to allow a free vote on any part of the bill.[25]

Trudeau proposed the Criminal Code be amended to provide that abortion be decriminalized if the pregnancy endangered the life or health of the mother, and was approved by a hospital Therapeutic Abortion Committee.

This amendment was in accordance with Trudeau's own personal views on abortion. According to a statement he made on September 25, 1976 in Edmundston, New Brunswick. He stated:

> "I consider the fetus, the infant in the womb is a living being, a being we must respect, and I do not think we can kill him arbitrarily. There are cases where killing is legal.... There are cases when it is legal to kill even an infant, but I am saying, when we kill... we must answer to society. That is why our Omnibus Bill requires three doctors... they are more competent than I, as regards to mental and physical health and I think it is a good law. It is easy for us men to be against abortion. I am against abortion. But I've never been pregnant, illegitimate or otherwise... I believe we must listen to

the woman's side of the story." [26]

Trudeau stated on the BBC program, *Panorama,* on July 13, 1970:

> *"You can't ask the totality of the people to accept my private morality as theirs. You have to make sure that the Criminal Code ... represents not the private morals of the people who happen to be in government at that time, but represents what the people feel to be the basic public standards of ethical conduct."*

That is, Trudeau introduced the concept that officials must not "impose" their "personal morality" (which always refers to traditional moral principles only) via legislation on moral issues. This was the concept he had learned during his studies in his earlier years and it remained with him throughout his political life. Although, Trudeau "personally" believed abortion to be wrong, knew it was killing, yet, as far as is known, never apologized for his actions which led to a massive increase in abortions. He persistently fought off all attempts to modify the legislation. In 1980, Trudeau still referred to his 1969 abortion amendment to the Criminal Code as a "reasonable" law. Not only did Trudeau change the law to permit easy access to abortion, but his Liberal government also facilitated the funding of abortions by way of the Medical Care Act (Now called the Canada Health Act) by requiring that each province decide which services would be necessary. Subsequently, all provinces decided that abortion would be funded as medically necessary.

Trudeau, above all, entrenched into Canadian politics the false concept that public officials must not "impose" their "personal morality" via legislation on moral issues. This led Fr de Valk to conclude:

> *"But of course Trudeau did impose his views on the public. His private, elitist view that morality has no place in law was bulldozed through Parliament and onto Canadian society. His private view was also that Canadians must be led to want his changes, not that they necessarily wanted them at the time - and Canadians, except for a small minority, were definitely not asking for the legalization of abortion.*
>
> *As a person who still thought of himself as a Catholic, Trudeau was tragically mistaken that such a position can be*

validly held by a Catholic politician. Pope John Paul II has made it clear that a politician cannot call himself a believing Christian and separate his political self from the Christian who has an obligation to act on the moral laws. Just last week the Vatican announced that on Nov. 5 the Pope will declare St. Thomas More the patron Saint of politicians. This sends a clear message to Catholic politicians that their joy should be in first remaining faithful to Christ, and the true good of the people, by always resisting pressure to politically co-operate with immorality - no matter what the consequences."[27]

Trudeau used deception to get abortion legalized through emphasizing "medical need." A "medical need" was when health problems occur with pregnancies. This was a rare occurrence even at that time.

Yet, well over three million pre-born children had lost their lives by 2016 and their mothers have suffered medical consequences of the abortion provision.

Catholics oppose the Omnibus Bill

The English Catholic press spoke out against the Omnibus Bill. *The Catholic Register* demanded that abortion be removed from the Omnibus Bill and called upon Catholic Liberal MPs to reject it. Fr. De Valk noted that Catholics and their hospitals "now felt themselves a beleaguered minority in all the provinces."

The Association of Catholic Hospitals vowed to fight the bill. Fr. John Mole, OMI, information officer for the Association of Catholic Hospitals which had 300 hospitals offering 35 % of Canada's health services, charged that:

"...that the legislation would divide the country at a time when Canadians needed unity. He accused Justice Minister Trudeau of having 'abused his office' by throwing the weight of his position behind the pro-abortion lobby. It was a 'sheer act of contempt' on Mr. Trudeau's part to have introduced the legislation without hearing from either the Canadian bishops or the Catholic Hospital Association."[28]

The Canadian Conference of Catholic Bishops issued a statement on the Omnibus Bill in February 1968. It opposed the law, citing among its consequences:

"This amendment of the law not only allows the direct and voluntary taking of an innocent life but opens the door to the broadest interpretations. Through the press, radio and television we are already getting expressions of public opinion that show a clear and alarming decline in respect for the life of the unborn. Some, for example, see the amendment proposed in the House of Commons as only the first step towards official recognition of 'abortion on demand'. Others believe that the amendment, as it stands, already provides the possibility for abortion in a very large number of cases." [29]

Parliamentary opposition to the bill came from the Quebec-based Créditistes, who spoke out courageously and strongly on the evils of this bill. The Liberals, many of whose members were Catholic, chose to remain silent.

The Jesuit Marcel Marcotte wrote in *Relations*, an intellectual monthly, as summarized by Fr. de Valk:

"Canada is definitely an Anglo-Saxon country with her umbilical cord still not cut. No sooner does Britain provide herself with new laws on divorce, homosexuality and even abortion, than the Canadian government follows hot on her heels, copying her slavishly. Are the ashes of political colonialism surreptitiously giving rebirth to a new, judicial, colonialism, he asked. Observing that the proposed abortion amendment was not merely one of a long existing tradition, he wondered at the end of the article, what purposes the Minister of Justice could have had in mind by burying abortion among all the other items in the omnibus bill. He noted as ominous that the Catholic Bishops had now refused to appear before the Commons Committee." (30)

When the Committee resumed its hearings in January 1968, various pro-life groups appeared before it.

One was Hamilton Right to Life, formed by Mr. and Mrs. Vincent Calzonetti. The chief spokesman was Dr. Gerald Quigley, chief of obstetrics at Hamilton's St. Joseph's Hospital. While opposing full abortion, he accepted abortion when the life or life expectancy of the mother was affected.

The London Society for the Protection of the Unborn, represented by Drs. L. de Veber, Jack Walters and W. Tillman, also appeared. The Catholic Hospital Association of Canada also testified. They asked that an exemption to permit hospitals the right to refuse to perform abortions. This was rejected.

The Canadian Conference of Catholic Bishops finally appeared before the Committee as well. When asked towards the end if abortion should be illegal under any circumstances, Fr. E.J. Sheridan replied:

> "As I understand your question, that abortion is illegal under any circumstances, no. The bishops have never been in favour of tightening the present law so as to exclude abortion. Abortion is permitted under our present Criminal Code, and certainly the bishops have never moved, do not wish to move, in the direction of tightening that. In other words, we do not believe that our moral principle must be enshrined in criminal law." (31)

Commenting on the proceedings of the Health and Welfare committee, Ottawa lawyer David Dehler wrote:

> "Anyone who followed the proceedings ... knows that the evidence before that Committee showed conclusively that : (1) according to modern medical and biological science the unborn child is from the moment of conception a human being; and (2) few, if any, medical indications exist for abortion and the rarest indications are rapidly disappearing with medical advance." (32)

On March 15, 1968 Pearson released Cabinet Ministers from their duties to campaign for the leadership of the Liberal party.

Further debate was then suspended while an election took place.

Trudeau becomes Liberal leader

In December, 1967 when Prime Minister Pearson declared his intention to resign as Prime Minister, Marc Lalonde, Michael Pitfield, and Trudeau's assistant, Eddie Rubin, all pushed for Trudeau to run for the Liberal leadership. Pearson supported this initiative as did Finance Minister and Deputy Prime Minister, Mitchell Sharp, who dropped out of the race to support Trudeau, and Joe Smallwood, Liberal Premier of Newfoundland who promised to deliver all 84 Newfoundland delegates to Trudeau.

Trudeau won the leadership race in 1968.

Omnibus Bill passes – abortion allowed

The debate on the Omnibus Bill is covered in detail in Fr. de Valk's book *Morality and Law in Canadian Politics*. Much of the following section is based on this book.[33]

After the election of the Liberal government, debate on the Omnibus Bill resumed in Parliament. Trudeau and his new Justice Minister, John Turner, both Catholics, confirmed the bill would continue. Supporters of the bill continued to promote it. They included the Canadian Bar Association, the Canadian Medical Association, and others such as the National Council of Women and the Presbyterian, United and Anglican Churches of Canada.

Opposing the legislation were the Catholic Church and the Lutherans, Mennonites, Pentecostals, Evangelicals, Mormons, Witnesses of Jehovah, the Greek Orthodox and the Jewish Orthodox.

Trudeau referred to the Wolfenden Report and made the inane statement that "the state has no business in the bedrooms of the nation" in his determination to remove moral issues from the Criminal Code. The purpose of the Criminal Code, however, is to uphold moral isssues whether prohibiting murder, fraud, sexual assault etc.

Dehler dissected Trudeau's sly statement on the government having no place in the bedrooms:

> *"Since government has no place in the bedrooms of the nation, murder in the bedroom is no longer a crime. Nor is rape or incest or assault."*

He noted that, to the contrary, the government had the duty to prosecute many bedroom crimes.

Dehler further writes:

> *"England's Abortion Act had a great impact in Canada. And to justify the changes in the criminal law dealing with gross indecency Trudeau used the Wolfenden Report and the British parliament's legislation to justify what Trudeau wanted to do in Canada. What was good for the United Kingdom, especially in matters sexual and in matters of life and death, must be good for Canada. Such was the Trudeau line."* [34]

When presenting the Bill C-150 legislation, the government introduced a vote allowing for the elimination of clause 18 which contained the proposed revisions on abortion. This proposed to eliminate all references to abortion in Bill C-150.[35]

In this vote, only 2 Liberals voted yes. They were John Reid (Lib-Lab, Kenora-Rainy River) and Ralph Stewart (L, Cochrane), while 85 Liberals voted against. The Progressive Conservatives were much more pro-life with 25 voting for it, and only 7 against. The NDP were against it, 15 voting against and 1 in favour. All 8 members of the Ralliement Créditiste, to their credit, voted for it.

Then the vote on the Omnibus Bill, C-150 came up.

The majority of Conservatives spoke out against it. Some of the comments were memorable. Walter Dinsdale (PC, Brandon-Souris) stated that Canada was embracing the Playboy philosophy. He quoted Dante:

"the hottest places in hell are reserved for those who in a period of moral crisis maintained their neutrality".

One NDPer, John Burton (Regina East) had the courage to denounce the legalization of the killing of the innocent.

The 14 Créditiste MPs, all Catholic, were firm in their convictions and quoted Pope and Bishops in rejecting abortion. Some comments were memorable. Roland Godin (C, Port-neuf) wondered whether:

"…the present government with its loathsome laws on divorce, on abortion, on homosexuality, is not simply a tool of a dreadful plot against our civilization".

Mr. Gauthier (C, Roberval) denounced the Liberals "who now claimed that the bill "was imposed upon them" and that "abortion is not so serious since the bill tends only to save the mother's life".

The Créditiste MPs attacked the Liberals endlessly. Mr. Fortin (C, Lotbiniere) said the Liberals:

"…seem to be seated on six inches of Lepage's glue, and we do not hear a peep out of them".

Mr. René Matte (C, Champlain) said:

"I want at least posterity, that is to say my own children and others, to know that we stood our ground … Sooner or later, we shall overcome."

Mr. Henri Latulippe (C, Compton) said:

> *"There are no more morals, there is no more conscience on the other side at the present time".*

The Conservatives and Créditistes proposed many amendments to the Bill. Some 50 amendments were proposed to clause 18 alone. Some were quite important. For example, one, allowing freedom of conscience, said:

> *"Nothing in this section shall be construed as obliging any hospital to establish a therapeutic abortion committee or any qualified medical practitioner to procure the miscarriage of a female person".*

Although this particular exemption had been granted in the UK and in US states legislation, it was rejected in Canada by the Liberals.

Indeed, all amendments were defeated, and in the end, Bill C-150 passed.

Trudeau's abortion amendment to the Criminal Code was passed in the House of Commons on May 9, 1969.

Of those who opposed Bill 150 because it legalized abortion among its many changes, 42 were Progressive Conservative. They were Alkenbrack, Bigg, Coates, Code, Crouse, Danforth, Diefenbaker, Dinsdale, Flemming, Forrestal, Grills, Gundlock, Hales, Howe, Lambert, Lasalle, MacEwan, MacInnes, McCutcheon, McGrath, McIntosh, McKinley, McQuaid, Marshall, Mazankowski, G. Muir, R. Muir, Nesbitt, Noble, Paproski, Peddle, Ricard, Rynard, Schumacher, Scott, Simpson, Southam, C. Stewart, Thompson, Thomas, Valade, and Yewchuk. The 10 Créditistes who opposed were Beaudoin, Caouette, Dionne, Fortin, Gauthier, Latulippe, Matte, Rodrigue, Rondeau and Tetrault.

To their perpetual disgrace, no Liberals or New Democrats voted against it. At the time of the vote, the Liberals had 155 members, the Progressive Conservatives had 72, the New Democratic Party had 22, and there was 1 Independent.

The Globe and Mail, in an editorial of May 14, 1969, praised the main evildoer:

> *"But it was the spirit of the bill that was important. It stepped boldly into a great many areas where legislators had never*

dared to step before. This is an essential spirit in our rapidly changing world…

The man to whom most of the honour must go is Mr. Trudeau."

Fr. de Valk writes:

"In a country with nearly half the population professing membership in the Roman Catholic Church, the new legislation on abortion passed easily and with a large majority. Taking into account the fact that, despite the claims of The Globe and Mail *and others, abortion was opposed not only by Catholics but by others, there ought to have been a comfortable majority against amendment of the law. Nevertheless the opposite was true."*

Fr. de Valk concluded:

"Opponents of legal abortions hold that abortion is an act of violence against (unborn) human life which is innocent of any misdeeds. They know that in western civilization, governments have traditionally, i.e. for two thousand years or more, condemned and suppressed such acts of violence. Now, within a matter of a few years some governments have suddenly decided to change the nomenclature and make these acts of violence "legal" in order to escape from what is admittedly a difficult situation. But in doing so these governments undermined the traditional use of language, and, above all, introduced into western society principles of behaviour which contradicted concepts essential to the older heritage generally known as the Judeo-Christian tradition. As this new view directly contradicts the traditional view it will ultimately force every person into one camp or another, because the new principles implied in the legalization of abortions will have a whole train of consequences, conscious and subconscious, foreseen and unforeseen, political and philosophical, personal and social. Together, these consequences will profoundly affect society and affect it, not for the better, but for the worse. Already, it is argued, abortion has contributed to confusing the virtue of compassion, the rights of women, the rights of unborn life, the rights of hospital personnel, the functions and rights of private and public

hospitals, the meaning of the Hippocratic Oath, the nature of the Criminal Code, the role of legislators and the purpose of law. To ask, then, in the name of a pluralistic society to accept such a situation is to ask, not for compromise on matters of secondary importance, but for surrender on a matter vital to society."

Lawyer Dehler makes some interesting points on the changes to abortion laws:

"Criminal law does not confer rights. Its exceptions do not confer rights. In fact the 'right' never did arise and still (as of 1980) does not exist. There is no 'right' to an abortion. There is no 'right' to do an abortion. There is only, and never forget: freedom from criminal prosecution when the unborn child is killed in hospitals by doctors with the consent of the mother and the approval of an abortion committee composed of other doctors who decide which child shall live or die; an abortion committee before which the child has no personal or legal representation, although, were his inheritance rights in question, the unborn child would be represented before the courts by the Official Guardian who protects the interests of children unborn as well as born; an abortion committee from which there is no appeal. Sweet justice in the just society."

Dehler further notes that abortion was permitted if it endangered the life or the very liberally interpreted "health" of the mother and only if approved by a committee of three doctors.

This definition of "health" would not last long. Dehler writes that John Turner, the Minister of Justice, made sure that the definition of "health" was very broadly interpreted. In a letter from his executive assistant Michael Hunter to the Ottawa Civic Hospital, on August 6, 1970, Hunter wrote:

"Mr. Turner is of the opinion that the word 'health' is very broad and may include physical, psychological or social health. He frequently refers to the definition given by the World Health Organization, which is as follows:

'Health is a state of complete physical, mental and social well-being and not merely the absence of disease or infirmity'."

Dehler then concluded that in less than 2 ½ years the word health no longer had the meaning the Health and Welfare committee gave it, and that Canada now had:

> *"In reality, abortion on demand sanctioned by the then Minister of Justice".*[36]

There was no significant public movement for the government to make changes in the abortion law. The law is a teacher and Canada's entire moral foundation was undermined by this so-called "private" decision for a woman to obtain an abortion with only minor difficulty. Abortion, however, is not a private matter since it deals with the destruction of the life of another human being. As such it is a matter of utmost public morality.

One of the consequences of the abortion amendment was that the birth rate plummeted in Canada to well below replacement level as abortions have risen astronomically each year. According to Statistics Canada, in 1972 11,200 abortions were performed. Today, in 2017, over 100,000 abortions take place each year. The removal of millions of future taxpayers from Canadian society as a result of abortion, has contributed to our aging population and our inability to sustain our retirement system and other social benefits. For example, in the 1970's there were seven workers for each retiree. Today there are approximately four. In 15 years, the ratio is expected to fall to just 2:1.

For a variety of reasons, but chief among them being the decriminalization of abortion, Canada today for the first time in history has a serious demographic imbalance. There are more seniors over 65 years of age than young people under fourteen years of age. This situation cannot be sustained and will need correction by radical immigration policies, which will create its own social and cultural challenges.

Chapter 3

Pro-life activism and constitutional initiatives during the 1970s

Trudeau centralizes power

Robert Fulford, a Toronto author, journalist and editor, wrote in the *National Post*:

"He (Trudeau) kept his own cabinet on a short leash and made free discussion of issues a punishable offense. More importantly, he withdrew most of the power of the ministers and centralized all authority in his office and the Privy Council office." [1]

In his memoirs, Trudeau justified himself, saying he needed more people to look after his correspondence and to respond to "uncontrollable situations". [2]

Bob Plamondon, a well-known Conservative writer, said of Trudeau's treatment of the Cabinet:

"Trudeau did not condone independent voices in cabinet and was ruthless when it came to protecting cabinet secrecy, warning his ministers that if the source of any leak of cabinet information were identified, 'the action taken would have to be merciless.' When reporters asked Trudeau if he was worried about dissension within Liberal ranks over his

leadership, he replied, 'If I found in my own ranks that a certain number of guys wanted to cut my throat I'd make sure I cut their throats first'." [3]

Over time Trudeau replaced the cabinet as a power chamber with his PMO (Prime Minister's Office). One of the powerful members of this group was Michael Kirby, known as Trudeau's "son-of-a-bitch". He also served as Deputy Clerk of the Privy Council and Secretary to the Canadian Cabinet for Federal Provincial Relations.

Below the PMO in Trudeau's power structure was the Privy Council Office (PCO). Michael Pitfield was the clerk for some years. He was a very close personal friend of Trudeau.

The corruption of parliamentary tradition, which gave dictatorial powers to the Prime Minister, has been continued by subsequent Prime Ministers, both Liberal and Conservative. These prime ministers have elevated and strengthened their personal power and control, rather than that of the people, the MPs or the government, and to a degree perhaps never before experienced in Canadian history.

Trudeau's attitude towards the democratically elected Members of Parliament was expressed in his quote:

"When they (opposition MPs) get out of Parliament, when they are fifty yards from Parliament Hill, they are no longer honourable members - they are just nobodys." [4]

In his response to criticism for this statement, Trudeau said he was:

"...not impressed by the atmosphere in the House", that "hours were squandered deliberating over minor details at the expense of much more important questions. I certainly did not have a great deal of respect for MPs who believed that truth lodged with whoever had the loudest voice." [5]

Plamondon writes:

"(Trudeau) viewed federal Liberals as exploitative, incompetent and corrupt. Hurling insults at the Liberal clan came easily to Trudeau, who claimed that "[t]he shameful incompetence of the average Liberal MP from Quebec was a welcome asset to a government that needed no more than a herd of performing donkeys to file in when the division

bell rang. The party strategists have but to find an acceptable stable master … and the trained donkeys sitting in the back benches could be trusted to behave"."[6]

Nonetheless Trudeau worried about some traditional MPs. He wrote:

"I had to be very circumspect from 1968 to 1972. Still somewhat shakily established at the head of the organization, I had to be constantly aware of the possible risks involved in ranging the more traditional Liberal members against me, and of provoking a rift between the two wings…I had to be on my guard all the time to maintain a careful equilibrium between progressive measures and more moderate ones."[7]

Trudeau further removed power from Parliament by creating agencies and commissions which worked independently of Parliament. During his period in power, he created 114 agencies and commissions.[8] In December, 1977, the chairman of the parliamentary committee on public accounts reported that the government owned wholly or partly, 380 corporations, not 360 as the government had previously reported. The government was involved in everything from airlines and railways to farming, lotteries, motels, soft drinks, oil and mines.

In his report on the 1976-77 fiscal year, Auditor-General J.J. Macdonnell said "in the majority of crown corporations audited … financial management and control is weak and ineffective".

Trudeau's interest in the constitution

Trudeau had a vision that a Charter of Rights should be a part of Canada's constitution. As far back as 1950, writing in the journal *Cité Libre*, Trudeau called for "the essential step of a declaration of rights entrenched in the constitution which would be binding on all Canadians and on all governments."

In 1962-1965 while teaching constitutional law and civil liberties at the University of Montreal, Trudeau argued during his lectures for a constitution which would include a Charter of Rights. His students later affirmed that which he taught in his lectures, was precisely what he implemented as Liberal Party leader.[9]

Trudeau's obsession with constitutional change increased once he became the Minister of Justice in September, 1967. He publicly declared that it was time for constitutional change, arguing for repatriation of the constitution, with an entrenched bill of rights (binding on both the federal and provincial governments) and an amending formula.

When he became Prime Minister in 1969, he appointed John Turner as his Minister of Justice, but stripped from him the constitutional file, which he reserved for himself in order to personally implement his vision of a new Canadian constitution.[10]

Special Joint Committee on Constitution set up in 1970

In 1970-1 the Liberal government announced constitutional hearings to be conducted by a Special Joint Committee of the Senate and of the House of Commons on the Constitution of Canada, chaired jointly by Senator Maurice Lamontagne and Mark MacGuigan, MP.

Pro-life groups present briefs to the Committee

The pro-life movement was involved in measures to protect the unborn from the very beginnings of the move to craft a new Canadian Constitution and the Charter of Rights.

Among the briefs presented to the Special Joint committee was that by the Chairman of the Toronto Right to Life Committee, Gwen Landolt.[11]

She requested that Canada's proposed new constitution "should guarantee explicitly the right to life of the unborn child." She noted that Canada "is already committed to do so as a signatory to the United Nations Universal Declaration of Human Rights." This declaration noted:

"3. Everyone has the right to life, liberty and the security of person.

7. All are equal before the law and are entitled without any discrimination to equal protection of the law."

She went on to explain that the use of the word "life" was further defined by the World Health Organization in 1948 when it stated that:

'utmost respect for human life was to be from the moment of conception on'.

Furthermore, in 1959, the United Nations adopted the Declaration of the Rights of the Child which again supplemented the Universal Declaration of Human Rights. The preamble to this declaration stated:

"Whereas the child, by reason of his physical and mental immaturity needs special safeguards and care, including appropriate legal protection, before as well as after birth"

This led her to conclude:

"Thus the representatives of most of the civilized nations of the world acknowledged that the being before birth was to be recognized as a 'child'."

The Declaration went on to provide:

"Principle 4 – The child…shall be entitled to grow and develop in health. To this end, special care and protection shall be provided both to him and to his mother, including adequate pre-natal and post-natal care.

Principle 8- The child shall be in all circumstances the first to receive protection and relief.

Principle 9-The child shall be protected against all form of neglect, cruelty and exploitation."

From this, Landolt concluded:

"If the child in the womb is entitled to grow and develop in health, and to be first in all circumstances to receive protection, it follows that his life cannot be taken from him.

In conclusion, Canada, as a member of the United Nations, has committed herself to uphold the rights of the unborn child. She should honour the commitment by guaranteeing these rights in her new constitution."

Landolt countered objections based on period of gestation or quickening resolutely by stating:

"These attempts to determine the humanity of the fetus are not only artificial and arbitrary, but they have been outdated by scientific discoveries. Geneticists now inform us that the human being receives its genetic code at the moment of conception. It is this genetic information which determines its characteristics, such as sex, colouring, blood type and its entire heritage. At this point, an absolutely unique human being, different from any other human being that has ever

or ever will be created, comes into existence. A being with a human genetic code is man."

She showed how from a legal point of view, the unborn child in Canada is clearly recognized as a human being:

"Canadian law on this point closely follows English law, which, since the eighteenth century, has steadily given more and more protection and recognition to the fetus. In Giddings vs the Canadian Northern Railway *(1920), the Saskatchewan Court of Appeal held that even though a child was unborn at the time of his father's death, he was nonetheless entitled to receive compensation for the loss of his father. In* Montreal Tramways vs Laveille *(1933), the Supreme Court of Canada held that a child deformed through injuries caused to him while still in the womb, was entitled to bring an action in the courts for wrongful injuries. Furthermore, in* Re Charlton *(1919), the Manitoba Court of King's bench held that an unborn child was entitled to participate in a gift left to all living children."*

She acknowledged that there were those who wanted abortion removed from the Criminal Code as a woman had a right to "control her own body." Yet, she pointed out, the flaw in this argument was that there were two bodies, not one, and the real question was whether a woman had a right to "privately decide to deny life to a separate and distinct human being." She noted that "it is no more a matter of private morality than is infanticide or other forms of killing."

Finally, she included in her submission, a summary of the current case law in Canada on the rights of the unborn child. It is significant that up to that time, the court decisions had been gradually providing extended protection and recognition to the unborn child, but this advancement came to an abrupt halt when Trudeau amended the law on abortion in the Criminal Code in 1969.

She closed by recommending financial aid, better housing, counseling and other remedies to expectant mothers.

Other pro-life groups from Ajax, Brougham, Ottawa and elsewhere presented strong and cogent arguments demanding that unborn Canadians be protected from conception onwards.

For example, Norine Finlay of the Ajax Right to Life Committee quoted various medical authorities in the United States that confirmed that the unborn child was a living human being. She lamented the fact that:

"Our present law in Canada, permitting abortion to pre-serve the life or health of the mother, sanctions the destruc-tion of human life. The law has given the decision in this weighty matter to a select group of individuals, the mother, her physicians and a hospital abortion committee. They an-swer to no one nor do they question whether this foetus is a human being or what rights this human being may have; their concern is the mother's rights and conveniences only. It is our contention that equal serious consideration must be given to the health and the life of the unborn person as is given to the mother."

Finlay closed in recommending that the right to life of the un-born be upheld and firmly defended as an integral part of our Ca-nadian Constitution. [12]

Betty Van Hezewyk, also from the Ajax Right to Life Committee noted:

"If the fundamental and primary right to life of all unborn citizens is being undermined then it would seem mandatory that this right be guaranteed in the constitution."[13]

Ita Venner, president of Nurses for Life, presented and said:

"The nurses' right for employment in hospitals must be pro-tected by a constitution. Nurses must not be forced by hospi-tal policy to assist in taking the life of a human being when such acts are contrary to the conscience of the nurses. I hope that in future discussions on abortion the role of the nurse and the psychological effects it may have on her will be taken into consideration." [14]

Mr. Fairweather, a member of the Special Committee, asked what the commission should do given that many Canadian are not pro-life and want abortion. To this came the reply from Ian Gentles, a professor of history at Glendon College, York University:

"The job of Canada's statesmen is not to be a reflection nec-essarily of what public opinion is at any given moment, but it is to represent what are the highest values in our civiliza-tion". Then he referenced the American Constitution which

guaranteed the right to life of every individual and equality before the law, even though many opposed this." [15]

Writing on the results of the Joint Committee, Dr. Dominique Clement, Will Silver and Dr. Daniel Trottier stated that the initiative was unsuccessful. However, they added that:

"...for the first time, there was a consensus that Parliamentary supremacy was not an obstacle to a bill of rights"

and continued that:

"...the report was a milestone in contributing to the erosion of Parliamentary supremacy as a cornerstone of Canada's political culture." [16]

The Pépin-Robarts Commission 1976

Stunned by the election of the Parti Québécois in 1976, Trudeau created in 1977, a *Task Force on Canadian Unity* better known as the Pépin-Robarts Commission from its two co-chairmen Jean-Luc Pépin, previously a federal cabinet minister, and John Robarts --- a former premier of Ontario. A panel of six prominent Canadians joined the two chairmen. The mandate of the Commission was rather elaborate but, in particular, they were to hold public meetings to seek out the views of individuals and groups on the question of Canadian unity and advise the federal government on the same issue. The Commission held stormy meetings in most of the important cities of Canada, received numerous briefs from individuals and groups across the country, and commissioned studies on specific subjects and consulted governments and important individuals in Canada. The sum total of its efforts was a massive documentation that the Commission distilled into three books entitled *Coming to Terms*, *A Future Together*, and *A Time to Speak*.

The conclusion of the Commission was that Canada needed "restructured federalism" in order to accommodate the twin realities of duality and regionalism in Canada. It recommended a redistribution of power, giving provinces residual powers, increased powers of taxation, preponderance on most aspects of immigration, powers to enable Quebec to preserve its French heritage, a reconstituted Senate, and an entrenchment of the Supreme Court in the constitution. No charter would be inserted into the supreme law and language would become a provincial jurisdiction.

Unable to agree with the main recommendations of the Report, especially with its decentralist thrust and its emphasis on "asymmetry", the Trudeau government shelved it permanently, as it had previously shelved much of the Laurendeau-Dunton Report on Bilingualism and Biculturalism. [17]

The Quebec historian, Frederic Bastien, wrote:

> *"Trudeau was furious. When he was handed the report, he threw it directly into the trash, to the surprise of his advisors."* [18]

Reaction to the legalization of abortion

For much of the 1970s, Christian groups tried to have the abortion amendment, now Section 251 of the Criminal Code, changed.

Various pro-life groups organized during this decade. They included the Right to Life Association of Toronto, formed by Gwen Landolt in 1971. This later became the Right to Life Association of Toronto and Area. The presidency was assumed in 1978 by Laura McArthur.

The political arm of the pro-life movement, at that time, The Coalition for the Protection of Human Life, partially accepted the seamless garment argument being promoted in the US and Canada claiming that issues of social justice, such as poverty, should be incorporated, along with abortion, as a seamless garment, all issues being of equal importance.

A brief to the Ontario government by the Coalition also compromised the pro-life movement's determination to protect all unborn human life.

This led to the formation of the political pro-life organization, Campaign Life Coalition (henceforth Campaign Life). The latter was organized by activists from all across Canada. Campaign Life was formed on May 25, 1978 in Winnipeg by Fr. Ian Boyd of Saskatoon, Robert S. Daoust of Longueuil, Kathleen M. Toth of Edmonton, Earl Amyotte of Windsor, Paul Dodds of Willowdale, Mrs. Jean Morse-Chevrier of Point-Gatineau, Dr. Jim McGettigan of Saskatoon, Paul Formby of Toronto, Pat Clarke of North Vancouver, Betty Greene of Vancouver, Al Selinger of Willowdale, Norah Ryan of Sudbury, Adrian Keet of Wingham, Cecelia Forsyth of Saskatoon, Shirley Reinhart of Calgary, Gerhard Herwig of

Surrey, Joe Campbell of Saskatoon, and Grace Cameron of Ottawa. The first president was Kathleen Toth and Gwen Landolt was the legal counsel. Jim Hughes became president in 1981.

Mary Ellen Douglas wrote that:

> *"These activists from all across Canada were dismayed by the Coalition for the Protection of Human Life and their endorsement of compromise positions."*

Another group that formed was the Alliance for Life, an organization with an educational focus, which began in Ottawa, then moved to Toronto. Numerous chapters of these organizations formed across the country during the decade.

Winifride Prestwich, a member of Campaign Life and a teacher at a private Toronto girls' school, accurately predicted that the fight against abortion was going to grow to be a fight against euthanasia and other moral issues.[19]

CWL opposes abortion

Besides the pro-life organizations, there were other groups resisting Trudeau and speaking out for the unborn. One was the Catholic Women's League.

In 1976 the CWL issued a statement on *The Right to Life - A Basic Norm of Society*. It noted that "innocent human life has a right to inviolability from the moment of conception to the moment of natural death". It noted that Canada, as a member of the UN, must respect the United Nations 1959 Declaration of the Rights of the Child which stated:

> *"Whereas the child, by reason of its physical and mental immaturity, needs special safeguards and care, including appropriate legal protection, before as well as after birth..."*

The CWL asked for two changes in federal legislation:

> *Amendment of the Canadian Bill of Rights RSC 1970 RC 44 as follows:*
>
> 1. *"It is hereby recognized and declared that in Canada there have existed and shall continue to exist without discrimination by reason of race, national origin, colour, religion or sex, or stage of maturity, whether born or unborn, the following human rights and freedoms..."*

2. *Removal of the word "health" from Section 251 of the Criminal Code."*

They wanted abortion to remain in the Criminal Code. [20]

The Abortion Caravan

Feminists became stronger during the 1970s, emboldened by the legalization of abortion and the many other changes brought by the Omnibus Bill.

Even though the 1969 amendment to the abortion law, in reality, resulted in abortion on demand, this was not sufficient for the radical feminists. They did not believe that a hospital therapeutic abortion committee should have the right to determine whether a woman should have an abortion, but rather, believed it should be her own personal decision.

Feminists had been emboldened by the 1963 book *"The Feminine Mystique"* written by U.S. author, Betty Friedan, which argued in support of women's unrestricted freedom, including abortion on demand. This book had sparked the second wave of feminism in Canada and the United States. Feminists believed that their time had come, and argued that all women supported their feminist policies, which included abortion on demand. This was a baseless claim, but nonetheless, was asserted by feminists.

The Vancouver Women's Caucus (1968-1971), allegedly on behalf of all Canadian women, began planning Canada's first national feminist protest.

In mid-April, 1970, a delegation of the Vancouver Women's caucus set out from Vancouver in a yellow convertible, a pick-up truck, and a Volkswagen bus with a black coffin strapped on the roof. This cavalcade travelled over 5000 kilometers from Vancouver to Ottawa, making 12 stops along the way to hold public meetings and encourage women to join their caravan.

The abortion caravan arrived in Ottawa on Mother's Day, May 9, 1970 with 500 women assembled to demand the legalization of unrestricted access to abortion services. They rallied on Parliament Hill for two days, and then burned Prime Minister Pierre Trudeau in effigy, in front of his official residence at 24 Sussex Drive. A black coffin adorned with coat hangers supposedly representing women who had died from self-induced or back-alley abortions was left at the Prime Minister's front door.

On May 11, approximately 18 women took seats in the gallery surrounding the House of Commons. Once seated, they chained themselves to their seats. Just before 3:00 p.m., one of the women rose from her seat in the gallery and began loudly reciting a prepared speech which interrupted debate on the floor of the House of Commons. Other women continued with the group's speech, as one by one they were removed by the House of Commons' security guards. They were heckled by onlookers as they were escorted from the House, which was shut down for half an hour during this demonstration.

Abortion Caravan Based on False Information

The main thrust of the abortion caravan was that "twelve thousand women" died annually from illegal abortions in Canada. Not to be outdone, the *Toronto Star* reported in 1970 that 2,000 Canadian women died annually from the 100,000 illegal abortions performed each year and about 20,000 had to be hospitalized with post-abortion complications. These statistics were outrageous falsehoods and were based on nothing more than imagination, and buttressed in the case of the Toronto newspaper by its enthusiasm for feminist demands.

It is noteworthy that Dr. Bernard Nathanson who was a co-founder of the U.S. National Abortion Rights Action League (NARAL), who later converted to the pro-life viewpoint, stated in his book *Aborting America*:

> *How many deaths were we talking about when abortion was illegal? In N.A.R.A.L. we generally emphasize the drama of the individual case, not the mass statistics, but when we spoke of the latter it was always "5,000 to 10,000 deaths a year." I confess that I knew the figures were totally false, and I suppose the others did too if they stopped to think of it. But in the "morality" of our revolution, it was a useful figure, widely accepted, so why go out of our way to correct it with honest statistics? The overriding concern was to get the laws eliminated, and anything within reason that had to be done was permissible. Statistics on abortion deaths were fairly reliable, since bodies are difficult to hide, but not all*

these deaths were reported as such if the attending doctor wanted to protect a family by listing another cause of death. In 1967, with moderate A.L.I.-type laws in three states, the federal government listed only 160 deaths from illegal abortion. In the last year before the Blackmun era began, 1972, the total was only 39 deaths. Christopher Tietze estimated 1,000 maternal deaths as the outside possibility in an average year before legalization; the actual total was probably closer to 500.[21]

In his book *The Hand of God: A Journey from Death to Life by the Abortion Doctor Who Changed His Mind*, Nathanson wrote:

We aroused enough sympathy to sell our program of permissive abortion by fabricating the number of illegal abortions done annually in the U.S. The actual figure was approaching 100,000 but the figure we gave to the media repeatedly was 1,000,000. Repeating the big lie often enough convinces the public. The number of women dying from illegal abortions was around 200-250 annually. The figure constantly fed to the media was 10,000. These false figures took root in the consciousness of Americans convincing many that we needed to crack the abortion law. Another myth we fed to the public through the media was that legalizing abortion would only mean that the abortions taking place illegally would then be done legally. In fact, of course, abortion is now being used as a primary method of birth control in the U.S. and the annual number of abortions has increased by 1500% since legalization. ... we were guilty of massive deception. [22]

It seems that "massive deception" was also fundamental to the Canadian feminists' abortion caravan.

The Abortion Caravan failed to change the abortion law in Canada. It remained unchanged for the following 18 years, until it was struck down by the Supreme Court of Canada under the Charter of Rights on January 28, 1988.

Pro-abortion groups increase their influence

Trudeau had strong support from the leading pro-abortion group at that time, CARAL (Canadian Association to Repeal the Abortion Law).

The media, in general, offered strong support for Trudeau's amended abortion law. They included prominent journalists, Pierre Berton; June Callwood; Adrienne Clarkson; Laura Sabia; and Doris Anderson, who endlessly promoted abortion in *Chatelaine* magazine, of which she was the editor.

However, there were a few media outlets, such as the *Toronto Sun*, which usually supported the rights of the unborn in its editorial policy.

The government of Quebec was a strong supporter of abortion. At a time when no state in the United States and no other province in Canada paid for illegal abortions with public money, Quebec did so. In 1978, over 25% of Quebec Medicare-funded abortions were illegal. The present situation was a moral/legal vacuum following in the wake of the Morgentaler trials, wrote George Peate in the *Montreal Catholic Times*, April 1980.

In July 1979, the Quebec Health Insurance Board (QHIB) temporarily discontinued payments for illegal abortions. Martin Laberge, President of the Regie de l'assurance Maladie, said in a January interview that his lawyers advised him that these 'office' abortions were 'criminal acts'. However, Social Affairs minister Denis Lazure, immediately reversed the QHIB policy decision, thus guaranteeing continued Medicare funding of the illegal abortions.

Several months later in December 1979, Laberge received a confidential opinion from the Quebec Justice Department advising that Medicare should pay for 'office' abortions.[23]

Trudeau uses taxpayer money to fund feminist groups

To promote his secular values, Trudeau enlisted the support of feminist groups and commenced funding them, by way of the Status of Women departmental agency established in 1976.

Family planning clinics, although their purpose was supposedly to provide information and assistance for birth control, were, in reality, centres for the promotion of abortion. Key among these groups was the Planned Parenthood Federation of Canada, which was generously financed by Health and Welfare Canada, as well as by provincial governments.

Among feminist groups funded by the federal government, the most prominent at that time was the National Action Committee on the Status of Women (NAC) started by Laura Sabia. Initially, Toronto Right to Life and the Catholic Women's League attended the meetings. However, when Sabia stated that abortion on demand and universal day care were core demands of the group, they withdrew from the organization.

NAC claimed 3 million members, which number was mere propaganda or puffery, not fact. The number was an aggregate of organizations across the country, some paying affiliation fees, and many not doing so, but whose members were counted as individual members of NAC, even though many of these members had no knowledge of this.

Each year NAC was given private meetings to press its demands with influential members of the Cabinet such as Monique Bégin, Minister of Health and Welfare, and Justice Minister Ron Basford.

Feminists went to Trudeau for money in 1972 and 1973 and he started funding them as a good example of "participatory democracy". Naturally they supported his agenda.

Women's Centres in many major cities were funded by the federal agency Status of Women. These Centres were virtual nerve centres for pro-abortion activity in Canada. For example, the Vancouver Women's Health Collective received $203,519 from both the federal and provincial governments between 1973 and 1977, and the New Woman Centre in Montreal received $500,000 between 1975 and 1978, when Marc Lalonde headed the Status of Women.

Trudeau formed the Federal Advisory Council on the Status of Women and appointed outspoken feminist Doris Anderson, editor of *Chatelaine Magazine,* to head the Council. It was an agency created to support government policies, since the government appointed as its members, Liberal supporters. Although one-third of the appointed Advisory Council members were pro-life, the majority was pro-abortion, and the Council promoted abortion as one of its policies.

Plamondon writes:

> *"Trudeau saw nothing wrong in using the public purse to advance the causes of his political allies – and, thereby his own electoral prospects. Indeed, Trudeau used taxpayer dollars to fund the sort of advocacy work normally undertaken by*

political parties. Groups such as the National Action Com-
mittee on the Status of Women went well beyond advocating
an end to discrimination; they campaigned for a wide range
of highly politicized social policy changes.

Trudeau institutionalized women's equality by appointing
a minister responsible for the status of women in 1971, and
then created the advisory council on the status of women in
1973." [24]

Trudeau passed the Canadian Human Rights Act which established the Canadian Human Rights Commission and the Canadian Human Rights Tribunal in 1977. They "created both a platform and industry for human rights in Canada".[25]

In 1978 Trudeau created the Court Challenges Program of Canada (CCP) "to provide financial assistance for important court cases that advance language rights. It initially funded challenges to Quebec's Bill 101. After the Charter was enacted, its mandate and scope grew dramatically."[26] The CCP was extended in 1982 by Prime Minister Mulroney to include legal challenges dealing with equality rights.

The program only funded left-wing organizations. As a result the challenges had a significant impact in changing Canadian values by using the courts to bypass Parliament.

Pro-life initiatives during the 1970s

After the passage of the Omnibus Bill in 1969, many hospitals throughout the country began setting up abortion committees to rule on abortions. Pro-life activists opposed these.

Fr. de Valk noted a number of areas in which pro-lifers sought to improve a deteriorating environment.[27] They were dissatisfied with the performance of many abortion committees in the hospitals – some of which approved every request received. Provinces began pressuring Catholic hospitals to do abortions.

Many lamented the coercion within hospitals. Occasionally nurses protested. One was Frances Martin who complained to the Ontario Human Rights Commission about being demoted at Henderson General Hospital in Hamilton because she refused to assist in abortions. The Commission ruled against her in a judgment that said it was "legal to attempt to coerce or penalize nurses who oppose abortions" because the latter was a legal procedure.

On a positive note, pro-lifers worked hard to help pregnant women so they would carry their children to birth. Louise Summerhill started Birthright in Toronto to promote an alternative to abortion. By 1973 it had 325 chapters throughout Canada and the United States.

Right to Life groups, concentrating on the educational aspects of abortion, started spreading to cities and towns throughout Canada. By 1974 there were 75 groups. They were federated nationally in the Alliance for Life whose headquarters was in Toronto. Its first president was Dr. Heather Morris, an obstetrician and gynacologist at Women's College Hospital in Toronto, who appeared frequently on television and radio shows in defence of the unborn child.

A few political leaders stood out in efforts to oppose the expansion of abortion. One was Joseph Borowski, a Manitoba MLA. He sacrificed his political career as a Minister of Transport in the NDP government of Manitoba in his efforts to stop coercion of abortion on women and to prevent publicly funded agencies from promoting abortion.

The million signature petition

In 1973, the pro-life groups under Alliance for Life gathered a petition of 352,000 signatures, requesting protection for the unborn child. This petition was presented to Prime Minister, Pierre Elliottt Trudeau. At that time, a prominent pro-life Conservative Member of Parliament, Douglas Roche (Edmonton South), recommended that in order to convince the Liberal government to positively amend the abortion law, it was necessary to present a petition with a million signatures.

This was precisely what the pro-life movement did to show beyond all doubt, that the people of Canada wanted the killing to stop. A petition demanding full protection for the unborn child was translated into many languages such as Greek, French, Slovak, German, Russian, Polish, Ukrainian, Hungarian, Chinese, etc. and distributed widely throughout Canada. It was distributed in churches, schools and clubs, and signatures were obtained by pro-life individuals from shoppers in local shopping centres. It was an intensive effort.

Within two years, 1,027,425 million signatures had been collected on the petition. This petition was tabled in the House of Commons on May 29, 1975. Never before in the history of Canada have so many people from different walks of life, ethnic origins, and religious affiliations, including those with no religious beliefs at all, joined together in such a deeply felt cause, i.e. civil rights and justice for **every** Canadian.

Presentation of the Petition to Parliament

At 12:15 p.m. on May 29, 1975, the petition arrived on Parliament Hill in a cavalcade of 10 cars – one for each province, carrying the petitions from each province, and flying the provincial flag. The cavalcade, which had toured downtown Ottawa, drove onto the Parliament grounds led by a kilted bagpiper.

The cavalcade of cars was met by 1,700 people cheering "*Vive la vie*", "Love Life" and "One (*Un*) Million".

After the 35 boxes had been carried into the House of Commons, there were brief speeches by pro-life leaders from English-speaking Canada and Quebec. At the end of the ceremony, in a moving moment, the crowd, composed of people from every part of Canada, all joined hands and sang "Oh Canada".

Leaders of Alliance for Life representing English speaking Canada and the Front commun pour le respect de la vie, representing the province of Quebec, met privately with Prime Minister Trudeau and Minister of Health and Minister Responsible for the Status of Women, Marc Lalonde to urge the protection of unborn children.

House of Commons – 3:00 PM

Liberal MP Ursula Appolloni (York South – Weston), presented the petition on the floor of the House of Commons.

Under the rules of the House, no speech at all may be made by an MP presenting a petition – this would include the reading of a lengthy petition – unless there is unanimous consent of the House. Such unanimous consent very rarely occurred, but it did in this case and Mrs. Appolloni read the petition, which was greeted with enthusiastic and prolonged applause.

During the entire day of May 29, delegates from across Canada lobbied MPs. The corridors leading to the offices of the Members of Parliament were thronging with people wearing their distinctive pro-life badge.

The effects of the petition

1. Pro-life MP Caucus formed:

The petition acted as a catalyst for MPs to form a pro-life caucus. It consisted of MPs from all parties. This caucus set a precedent in that there had never before been members of parliament formed into a group from all parties. This caucus has continued to function throughout the many parliaments that have existed over the past four decades.

2. The Establishment of a Committee to Review the Abortion Law:

In the weeks following the presentation of the pro-life petition, MPs continued to question the Liberal government for its response to the petition.

On September 29, 1975, four months after the one million signature petition had been presented to Parliament; the government announced the establishment of a committee to review the operation of the abortion law.

The Terms of Reference set for the Committee were that it was "to conduct a study to determine whether the procedure provided in the *Criminal Code* for obtaining therapeutic abortions is operating equitably across Canada." The Committee was asked to report on the operation of the law, but not make recommendations on the underlying policy.

The members of the Committee were Sociologist Professor Dr. Robin F. Badgley, Chairman and Denyse Fortin Caron, a lawyer from Montreal. The third member of the Committee was the notorious Dr. Marion G. Powell, a well-known pro-abortion activist and a member of the Association of Doctors for the Repeal of the Abortion Law. The addition of Dr. Powell to the Committee was a sly move by the Liberal Government to ensure that the report would not be a neutral analysis of the abortion law, but would be directed toward providing evidence to widen the abortion law.

The Catholic Women's League in its 1976 statement on abortion took note of the fact that the members of the Badgley Committee were not impartial and demanded that the committee have a strong pro-life person to counterbalance the pro-abortionists and called for public meetings and making data received available to the public.[28]

The Committee's report was submitted to the government in January, 1977. Not surprisingly, the Committee reported that there was "considerable confusion, unclear standards and social inequity" involved with the practice of the current abortion law and that there was "unequal access to abortions" in Canada.

The Report did admit, however, that there was little consensus in Canada about the abortion law or whether steps should be taken to amend the law. The Report did say, however, "most people across Canada from whom information was obtained, did not wish to see abortion removed from the *Criminal Code*". The Report also stated that although there was limited support among the medical profession for the hospital therapeutic abortion committee system, "there was no extensive support among physicians for any other option".

As a consequence of this lack of consensus, no action was taken by the federal government to amend the abortion law. The Badgley Report was ignored.[29]

Dehler challenges abortion law

David Dehler, an Ottawa lawyer, challenged the abortion law in the Ontario courts. The court's decision in that case became a crucial component when the Constitution with the Charter of Rights was repatriated to Canada.

Previously, he had successfully brought several *ex parte* applications before the Ontario courts seeking injunctions against the performance of abortions.

In his court challenge on the abortion law before the Ontario Superior Court in 1979, Mr. Dehler argued:

"*1. Parliament does not have a constitutional mandate to authorize the killing of an innocent human being.*

2. The courts must intervene when a law permits the killing of an innocent human being – on the grounds that there is a natural law of justice that supersedes any parliamentary authority.

3. An unborn child is a human being and this is an undisputed question of fact."

In September 1979, Mr. Justice Sidney Robins rejected these arguments, saying:

"Accepting as a fact the conclusion the plaintiff seeks to establish by testimony at trial, that is, that a foetus is a human being from conception, the legal results obtained remain the same. The foetus is not recognized in law as a person in the full legal sense...The cases here and elsewhere demonstrates that the law has selected birth as the point at which the foetus becomes a person with full and independent rights."

Dehler brought an appeal before the Ontario Court of Appeal. The latter rejected his appeal, accepting the reasons put forward by Sidney Robins in the lower court.

Dehler then applied to the Supreme Court for Leave to Appeal. The Supreme Court denied his application.

Dehler published a book in 1980 entitled *The New Canadian Ethic: Kill our Unborn Children*. In that book he incorporated details of his lawsuits, as well as a submission by Dr. Andreas J. Nuyens, an Ottawa physician specializing in obstetrics and gynecology, which identified the stages of development of the unborn child from conception to natural birth. [30]

Chapter 4

Trudeau pushes the Constitution 1978-1980

Canadian Bar Association supports Constitutional Reform

Trudeau's efforts for constitutional reform were bolstered in 1978 when the Canadian Bar Association, Committee on the Constitution, whose chairman was Jacques Viau, released a research study entitled *Towards a New Canada*. (1) The executive vice-chairman and director of research was Gerard V. La Forest, who was later appointed to the Supreme Court of Canada. The Preamble identified as fundamental rights:

> *"Dedication to the rights of the individual so that all may be free to develop their full potential without discrimination on grounds of sex, race, national or ethnic origin, colour or creed. Closely related to this is the principle of freedom under law."*

The document went on to say that individuals required freedom of thought, conscience, opinion, information, assembly, association, speech, universal suffrage, and privacy. Otherwise there is no proper operation of the supremacy of Parliament. Therefore there is no conflict between entrenching these rights and the supremacy of Parliament.

This reasoning, to say the least, was obscure since entrenching rights in a constitution undermines Parliamentary supremacy. Parliament as a result of this reform would no longer have the final say on such rights.

Canadian Unity information office

In 1978, the federal government established the Canadian Unity Information Office to promote not so much national unity, but rather a new constitution. The head of the Unity Office was Trudeau's good friend and fellow believer in the modernization of Quebec, Jean-Louis Gagnon. That year, the Canadian Unity Information Office published *Notes on Canadian Federalism.*

For example, Note 6 – Challenges facing Canadian Federalism notes:

"A country such as Canada cannot, however, permit itself to become a weak, unstable alliance of small political units in which the central government has insufficient power to influence an increase in the standard of living of all citizens and to redistribute revenue among the provinces and among the citizens in an equitable manner.

An equally great challenge is to provide constitutional guarantees of the rights of Canadian citizens, including their language rights."

Note 11 entitled: The Constitutional "Status Quo" was interesting in that it stated:

"In a meeting of the provinces in 1967, called the Confederation of Tomorrow Conference, the federal government embarked on a program of consultation with the provincial governments, which lasted from 1968 to 1971. During this period, the federal government presented the provinces with a plan for amending the constitution, which include, among other things, new proposals concerning the distribution of powers and a new division of responsibilities in the field of social security.

These meetings led to the Victoria Conference in 1971 at which the federal government, in addition to proposing the "patriation" of the constitution from England and an amending formula, put forward a set of proposals provid-

ing for amendments in the areas of official languages and fundamental rights. This set of proposals also guaranteed provincial participation in the selection of judges for the Supreme Court of Canada.

Since the Victoria Conference, the federal government continued to take steps to bring about changes in the constitution." [2]

During the 1979 campaign, Trudeau had told a large Toronto rally that he would bring the constitution home even if it meant going over the provincial leaders' heads and seeking approval through a national referendum. [3]

Plamondon wrote that Trudeau, who pushed the constitution in the 1979 election, was told that the public was fed up with the constitutional question. [4]

The Liberals lost the 1979 election for the first time since 1962. They held 114 seats to become the Official Opposition in Parliament. The Progressive Conservative Party of Canada under Joe Clark won 136 out of 282 seats to form a minority government. [5]

That Parliament, however, did not last long as Prime Minister Joe Clark lost a vote of confidence over his proposed budget. This budget included an increase in gas prices by eighteen cents a gallon as well as increases in taxes on tobacco and alcohol, all deeply unpopular. [6]

In the 1980 election which followed, pro-life groups and individuals called for a pro-life government. For example, at a gathering of the Trans-Canada Festival celebrating Faith, Freedom and the Family, a Baptist pastor, Ken Campbell, president of Renaissance, the Voice of Canada's Moral Majority, reaffirmed its commitment to the family, the institution of marriage, the political and judicial systems and the dignity and worth of the individual. Renaissance had set up a commission under Dr. Blair Shaw, which received more than 20,000 submissions, then wrote a report called *Report on the Family*. A manifesto resulting from it had many recommendations, including:

"3. Seek and support legislation aimed at reversing the growing callous influences in our society of dehumanizing mentality toward the unborn child, the aged, the handicapped and the infirm".

It mailed this manifesto to all candidates in the February 1980 election as well as to 100,000 homes of the Moral Majority constituency in Canada. [7]

Unfortunately, this tremendous effort to promote a strong pro-life government failed. It failed probably because, as noted above, of the deep dissatisfaction with the budget and new taxes which was a priority with the voters.

Liberals regain majority in 1980

In the following 1980 election campaign, Trudeau said nothing about the constitution, as he knew no one wanted it. His tactic worked.

Although Trudeau won a majority with 147 seats, it is arguable that the election provided him with a mandate to undertake constitutional renewal. This is because Trudeau did not have national support since his party held only 2 of the 77 seats west of the Ontario border. His Quebec MPs represented 50% of the Liberal caucus, at a time when Quebec was home to only 27% of the nation's ridings. The PCs came second with 103 seats and the NDP came third with 32. Even without full support from across Canada, Trudeau was determined to proceed with a new constitution based on his majority of seats. It was obviously irrelevant to him from where the seats came, i.e. Central Canada representing only Ontario and Quebec. [8]

In order to proceed with his constitution, Trudeau had to first deal with Quebec, which was led by popular separatist leader, René Lévesque, who had called for a referendum to separate Quebec from Canada.

With an 85.6% turnout in the referendum of May 20, 1980, 59.56% of Quebec's voters rejected sovereignty-association. It was a great victory for Trudeau, but not his last. Trudeau wrote:

"I knew that we had to move fast to use the moral imperative of the referendum victory to settle the constitution question"[9]

Within 24 hours of the federalist victory in Quebec, Trudeau dispatched his Justice Minister Jean Chrétien on a whirlwind tour of the provincial capitals. He wanted to see what kind of deal the Premier would accept. It should be noted that this "promise" of constitutional change made by Trudeau as well as Chrétien never talked about a charter. There was no mandate to push a charter.

Chrétien worked hard to finalize a deal. On June 7, 1980 the premiers met with Trudeau. He proposed "that constitutional negotiations be approached in two stages. First we wanted "a peoples' package" – consisting of patriation and a charter of rights – to be negotiated, and then we would get down to talking about the "politician's package", the division of powers between the federal government and the provinces."

Also, in June 1980, Trudeau met the United Kingdom Prime Minister Margaret Thatcher and told her of his plans to repatriate the constitution. Plamondon writes:

> "While Thatcher gave indications of support, Trudeau had failed to inform her of his plans to include a charter of rights in the patriation package, or of the likely provincial resistance. Later she remarked, "How can you expect me to be enthusiastic about your charter when we are against one?" The British Government was not amused and leaked news of its displeasure to The Globe and Mail. The Westminster Parliament Committee on Foreign Affairs under Sir Anthony Kershaw warned that the British Parliament was under no obligation to pass legislation requested by Ottawa unless there was agreement from the Canadian provinces." [10]

The Quebec historian Frederic Bastien writes that the British Prime Minister, Margaret Thatcher, was determined to work closely with Prime Minister Trudeau and not with provincial premiers and other interest groups. She did not want to be accused of interfering in the internal affairs of the country. The MPs in the UK would think differently, as noted below. [11]

By September 7, 1980 with the premiers opposing the package, Trudeau said the federal government would act unilaterally.

Trudeau pressed hard to ensure the Liberal caucus would support him and do as they were told. He met the caucus on September 17, 1980:

> "I explained to them (caucus) as well that the more we expanded the Charter of Rights, the more troubles we would have with the premiers. Some of the premiers believed very strongly in the British view of the parliamentary system, which holds that the legislature must always have the last

word on everything. A charter deviates from that, by setting out some basic rights that the courts can uphold and that no legislature can take away. My answer was always that the British system works for Britain, but we are not a unitary state like Great Britain and we have a lot of minorities. But the question now was whether a full charter was what we should unilaterally seek from Britain. We obviously had to have protection of the Official Languages Act and some other elements of a charter such as we had agreed to in Victoria, back in 1971. But the more rights we protected, the more we would be encroaching on parliamentary supremacy and therefore obliging the provinces as well as Parliament to modify some of their laws accordingly.

I was cautious about this, because I didn't want to risk going too far, leaving the caucus behind. But almost unanimously, the caucus wanted to go for a full charter. (12)

What is noteworthy about the Liberals in 1980 was that, according to Kathleen Toth, president of Campaign Life, there were forty-two pro-life Liberals who should have opposed Trudeau right from the start.(13)

A day later, Trudeau met the Cabinet.

"The key issue in the Cabinet was whether to entrench the charter of rights. But like the caucus, almost without exception the Cabinet felt that minority-language education rights must be entrenched in a new constitution. And once we had made the decision to impose minority-language education rights, then logically our position had to be to impose the full charter. As a result, the charter that emerged from these Cabinet discussions was significantly expanded from the limited charter that had been accepted so long ago at the Victoria conference in 1971." (14)

With his majority government and the full support of his cabinet and caucus, Trudeau now knew it was the time to press for an entrenched Charter of Rights. He did so because he firmly believed the courts would protect the rights of minorities from the majority. Ironically, his determination to protect the rights of the minority from the majority did not prevent him from using his majority in Parliament to overcome the strong objections of most

Canadians from across the country to his constitutional proposal.

Throughout 1980, a number of groups were mobilized against Trudeau's proposed constitution and charter because it failed to protect the unborn. Among these were the Knights of Columbus.

In the spring of 1980 the Saskatchewan Knights of Columbus passed a resolution that they would hold back that portion of their federal taxes which would be used to cover abortions and abortion services. Pro-abortionists demanded that they be prosecuted. The Minister of National Revenue, William Rompkey, who was opposed to abortion, said "he would be employing the normal process to collect the taxes".

In June 1980, Campaign Life president Kathleen Toth wrote to the Canadian Conference of Catholic Bishops requesting funding for her organization. She noted that there were now two political action pro-life groups in Canada who, with different strategies, were both:

> "...genuinely concerned with establishing legal protection for every innocent human being from conception to natural death".

Toth notes that having two groups:

> "has become doubly confusing for the pro-abortion forces, who must now track the activities of both groups."

She then mentioned the many activities in which Campaign Life was involved, including provincial elections, providing a brief for the Hall Commission on Health, and promoting a federal "Liberals for Life" movement. She closed by asking the bishops to split the money they plan to give to the Coalition for the Protection of Human Life with Campaign Life.[15]

Remi de Roo, Bishop of Victoria replied that he would consult with his budget advisors before giving any reply. The proposal was then rejected.

The *Toronto Sun* was a major Toronto paper that opposed Trudeau's charter. On July 8, 1980, an editorial said:

> "No Prime Minister in our history has Pierre Trudeau's record on human rights...
>
> Who was the P.M. who brought in the War Measures Act

– the greatest peacetime violation of human rights in Canadian history? Who has used the Official Secrets Act to go after the press whose freedoms Mr. Trudeau expressed such concern for?

Whose administration used the Official Secrets Act to persecute and break a citizen (Peter Treu) and drive him out of Canada? Whose government has even ordered escapers from communism deported back to oppression? [At least one, Alicia Wiercioch, chose suicide rather than return to Poland.]

And when the great opportunity came to fight for human rights in the war against Hitler, who ducked military service, dropped a couple of years off his age, and disappeared into a U.S. university after campaigning against conscription?

We all know who. No, when Trudeau gets sentimental about human rights, it is like a crocodile weeping. Be careful. Someone is trying to pull a fast one." [16]

Pro-abortion groups become more vocal

In August 1980, Beverley Baines, Assistant Professor, Faculty of Law, Queen's University prepared a paper for the Advisory Council on the Status of Women, entitled *"Women, Human Rights and the Constitution"*. Baines reviewed previous cases in Canada and concluded:

"the absolute necessity of effectively worded legislation if women expect legal protection of their human right to equality".

She recommended entrenchment of the equality clause because courts will treat a constitutional law as more important and therefore as more binding than in a Canadian bill of rights. [17]

In November 1980, the Liberal appointed Advisory Council on the Status of Women submitted its recommendations to Jean Chrétien, who accepted them. According to a Canadian Press release dated November 18, 1980, the purpose of these recommendations was to prevent "fetuses from having protection from the Charter".

Trudeau sets up constitution team

To facilitate a new constitution, Trudeau set up a constitutional team, whose members included Pitfield, Lalonde, and Michael J. L.

Kirby. This team reflected Trudeau's impatience with the federal government's conciliatory stance towards the provinces during the late 1970s.

The Charter of Rights was drafted by Deputy Minister of Justice Roger Tasse.[18] He would tirelessly assure Liberals, the churches and the public that the disastrous effects of a charter predicted by many good people would not happen.

At the federal–provincial meeting which took place in September 1980, the premiers were divided among themselves, with most insisting on greater decentralization. Newfoundland premier Brian Peckford stated that he preferred Lévesque's vision of Canada to Trudeau's, which apparently meant that he favoured decentralization to the prime minister's centralization. Lacking provincial support, Trudeau met his caucus and asked whether they would go with "the full package" even if the provinces hesitated. They enthusiastically agreed. On 2 October he told the country that because of the Premiers' lack of agreement, he was forced to act unilaterally to patriate the constitution. Canadians needed to assume "responsibility for the preservation of our country." The great debate that followed split parties: Clark's Conservatives vigorously fought the plan, while Ontario Conservative premier William Davis and New Brunswick Conservative premier Richard Hatfield supported it. The federal NDP were not unanimous; four Saskatchewan MPs sided with the province's NDP Premier Allan Blakeney, who opposed it on the traditional British conservative argument that Parliament must be supreme in the British system and not limited by the courts.[19]

Chrétien continued to speak in favour of a bill of rights. At the annual constituency dinner in Etobicoke-Lakeshore riding in Ontario, Jean Chrétien said that:

> *"A Bill of Rights must be entrenched in the Constitution if the rights Canadians have acquired over the years and have come to expect are to be protected...Chrétien said he was proud of the freedom, opportunity and justice available to all Canadians and would not want to see these compromised."* [20]

Just as if Canadians didn't already have these rights.

The Liberals started heavy publicity campaigns in support of their constitution and charter. The Hon. Jim Fleming, Minister of State (Multiculturalism), stated that it was important to have a federal publicity campaign to sensitize public opinion to the need for constitutional reform. The campaign stressed that individuals must give no government the right to reduce the basic rights of the individual. He identified these rights as "equal access to education, to medical care, to earn a living as a worker, a professional or in business". Without an entrenched bill of rights, these rights would become the "object of bargaining among various provincial governments". The Liberals claimed the campaign had a positive effect, as a Gallup poll, taken October 8, 1980 claimed that 72% wanted equal access to job opportunities across Canada. (21)

The opposition in Ottawa criticized the campaign. For example, in the House of Commons debates, for Tuesday, October 7, 1980, Lorne Nystrom (NDP Regina-Qu'Appelle) commented on sections 20, 23, 31, 42 and 46 of the charter. He mentioned the power of the federal government to manipulate public opinion:

> *"I have been in politics long enough to know that money can manipulate public opinion. This summer (1980) I saw an advertising campaign launched by the federal government. They spent $6 million rewarding a lot of their friends in the advertising business, talking about Canada and the constitution. That advertising program will be increased. I understand the unity office is increasing its budget from $10 million to over $30 million. It is planning another major advertising program in the country. It is wrong, because they are advertising a single proposal, not a government law or government program."*

In the past the government did not do this. Nystrom noted that when Judy LaMarsh was secretary of state she explained why she did not put on an advertising program to promote the Canada Pension Plan. He said:

> *"Her response was that it would not be proper, that it was a government proposal which had not been passed by Parliament. She indicated that it was not the law of the land and therefore the government had no moral right to advertise a proposal, which in fact was a partisan proposal of the Government of Canada."* [22]

Trudeau and his Liberals could care less.

Trudeau presents Resolution on the Constitution Oct 2, 1980

As referred to above, on October 2, 1980, Prime Minister Trudeau issued a Release on the proposed constitution. He lamented that the eleven first ministers had failed to reach agreement on the new constitution. To overcome this, he had submitted a Joint Resolution which, if approved, would lead to a new amending formula and would strengthen the rights of every Canadian. Thirdly, it would enshrine the principle of equalization. He closed by saying:

"Freed of the paralysis of the past, with our constitution home, with our full independence beyond question, with our rights and freedoms guaranteed, the process of reform and renewal can truly proceed." [23]

The Prime Minister presented the Proposed Resolution for a Joint Address to her Majesty the Queen respecting the Constitution of Canada.

Among its important points were:

1. *The Canadian Charter of Rights* and Freedoms guarantees the rights and freedoms set out in it subject only to such reasonable limits as are generally accepted in a free and democratic society with a parliamentary system of government.

2. Everyone has the following fundamental freedoms:
    a. Freedom of conscience and religion
    b. Freedom of thought, belief, opinion and expression, including freedom of the press and other media of information;
    and
    c. Freedom of peaceful assembly and of association

3. Every citizen of Canada has, without unreasonable distinction or limitation, the right to vote in an election of members of the House of Commons or of a Legislative Assembly and to be qualified for membership therein

4. Everyone has the right to life, liberty and security of the person and the right not to be deprived thereof except in accordance with the principles of fundamental justice.

5. Everyone has the right not to be subjected to any cruel and unusual treatment or punishment.

6. (Everyone has the right to equality before the law and to the equal protection of the law without discrimination because of race, national or ethnic origin, colour, religion, race or sex.

7. The guarantee in this Charter of certain rights and freedoms shall not be construed as denying the existence of any other rights or freedoms that exist in Canada, including any rights or freedoms that pertain to the native peoples of Canada. [24]

Many of these proposals were subsequently questioned by individuals supporting the pro-life position, concerned about the protection of unborn children.

On October 6, 1980, Jean Chrétien, Minister of Justice, spoke on constitutional reform. He noted the many earlier attempts to repatriate which had failed because of failure to agree on an amending formula. He mentioned Trudeau wanting to consult the provinces and the agreement of the Conservatives in doing so.

Chrétien cited the concessions the federal government was prepared to make in areas such as jurisdiction over family law, fisheries, management and development of offshore resources, communications, and equalization payments.

The federal government was willing to place the Supreme Court in the constitution and "would give the provinces a say in the appointment of Supreme Court judges".

Chrétien cited the reason for failure as:

> *"The reason we did not reach agreement was that provincial governments attempted to bargain the rights of Canadians against more powers for the provinces. We were prepared to negotiate powers of governments, but we would not negotiate people's rights against powers for government."*

This statement by Chrétien was clearly a mischaracterization of the actual situation. He then cited three reasons for acting unilaterally:

> 1. *If Quebec voted for federalism, there would be constitutional renewal – individual and language rights would be protected everywhere*

2. *Create a momentum for change – once the constitution was home, change could be made as and when necessary*
3. *Canadians want politicians to make Canada work the way it can and should*

For these reasons he brought forward a motion to repatriate the constitution and entrench a charter of rights and freedoms. Chrétien quoted the Constitutional Committee of the Canadian Bar Association, summarizing what has been noted above. He also noted:

> *"It is true that there are now non-constitutional Bills of Rights at the federal and provincial levels. But these are mere legislative directions to the courts as to how legislation is to be interpreted. Constitutional entrenchment should encourage courts to take a stronger stand to protect fundamental rights."*

Chrétien noted that provinces had agreed to be bound by the International Covenant on Civil and Political Rights and so therefore should not object to being bound by a Canadian Charter of Rights and Freedoms. He did not mention that the UN treaties protected the family, the supremacy of God and the right to own property – all absent from the proposed charter.

Chrétien spoke extensively on French language rights across Canada in schools and in the operation of the federal government, as well as on equalization payments, to share the wealth of Canada.

He closed by stating that the Parliament of Canada had no legal impediment to asking the Parliament of Great Britain to amend and patriate the Canadian constitution. This was not true.

Provinces go to court Oct 14, 1980

A few days after Trudeau's announcement, Manitoba, Newfoundland and Quebec declared that Trudeau's resolution was illegal and brought court challenges against it. [25]

In a CTV question period, Chrétien attacked the Premier of Manitoba, Sterling Lyon:

> *"I think that there are some provinces, there is very few of them who have opposed the charter of rights in principle. I think that is Mr. Lyon, who says he does not want any char-*

ter of rights at all, but the other premiers are not there to attack the charter of our rights and the concept of enshrining the basic rights of the Canadian constitution."

He further claimed:

"The people want to enshrine a charter of rights in the Canadian constitution. All the polls have been quite constant of that, it's always above 80%. The problem we're all facing is that nobody likes the process, neither do I." [26]

Nor, it turned out, did Canadians understand the implications of a charter which was to transfer power from Parliament to the courts.

Senate & Commons Committee on Constitutional Reform established

On October 29, 1980 the Liberal government announced that a House of Commons and Senate Committee on Constitutional Reform was to be established to review the charter of rights.

Eight Liberals, five Conservatives and two NDPers from the House of Commons and ten Senators were appointed to the committee. The Liberal MPs were Robert Bockstael, Colin Campbell, Eymard Corbin, Jean La Pierre, Serge Joyal, Bryce Mackasey, Ron Irwin and George Henderson. The Conservative MPs were Jake Epp, David Crombie, Jim McGrath, John Fraser and Perrin Beatty. The NDP members were Stanley Knowles and Lorne Nystrom.

Mr. Joyal, Liberal MP from Montreal, and Senator Harry Hays from Calgary were appointed Joint Chairmen of the committee.

The committee was instructed to present its report on December 9, 1980. [27]

On November 16, the mandate of the Senate House of Commons Special Joint Committee on the Constitution of Canada was extended until February 6, 1981. Individuals and groups were invited to make submissions to the committee. [28]

Coalition for the Protection of Human Life brief to the Special Joint Committee

On November 19, the Coalition for the Protection of Human Life presented a brief to the Special Joint Committee. It recommended changes in sections 1, 2, 7 and 15 of the proposed charter.

Regarding section 2 it recommended:

Everyone has the following fundamental rights and freedoms:

a. *"The right to life, liberty, and security of person and property, and the right not to be deprived thereof except in accordance with the principles of fundamental justice."*

Regarding section 15, it requested "everyone" be defined to mean "every living human being from the time of conception onward".

A member of the Coalition for the Protection of Human Life, Denyse Handler, said:

"Women's groups campaigned in the early part of the century to be recognized as "persons' before the law and now want to deny that same right to unborn children." [29]

Canadian Conference of Catholic Bishops did not present brief

The General Secretary of the CCCB Fr. Dennis Murphy had retained the legal services of Joseph Magnet, Q.C., constitutional lawyer and professor at Ottawa University to prepare the CCCB brief on the Charter of Rights. Fr. Murphy advised Campaign Life that Mr. Magnet had been highly recommended to them by Trudeau himself. It is probable, therefore, that Magnet was a supporter of the Liberal party.

The brief prepared by Magnet, which was never presented to the Parliamentary Committee on the Constitution for reasons discussed below, was most curious. It included a provision recommending the entrenchment of bilingualism in the Charter as proposed by the Quebec bishops. It did not, however, make any reference to the protection of the life of the unborn child - despite the fact that this was a major tenet of the Catholic faith.

When questioned on this omission by Gwen Landolt, Magnet responded that it was not necessary to include it in the brief, since the abortion law would not be affected by the proposed Charter.

Magnet confirmed his interpretation of the Charter on the abortion issue in a letter dated March 19, 1981 addressed to the General Secretary of the CCCB, Fr. Dennis Murphy. He stated:

"The Court was clear that abortion legislation is legislation which criminalizes 'socially undesirable conduct'...; it is

not legislation which establishes or denies the right to life to anyone...

s.26 of the Charter does not prevent Parliament from creating new rights...Parliament could create a 'right to life' for the unborn, even though the unborn do not presently have that right. Parliament could do this by criminalizing all abortions, including therapeutic abortions, as socially undesirable conduct subject to punishment.'

'The mother's right to therapeutic abortion exists by ordinary federal enactment, s.251 of the criminal code, not by any constitutional provision...as the mother's right to therapeutic abortion is given by ordinary federal statute, it may be taken away by ordinary federal statute'." [30]

This interpretation by Magnet was apparently not based on his personal support for abortion, since, a few years later, in 1989, Magnet wrote a strong dissent as a member of the Law Reform Commission against weakening the protection of the unborn child. Further, in January 1991 Magnet gave an eloquent plea for protection for the life of the unborn child before the Senate Legal and Constitutional Committee when it reviewed Prime Minister Brian Mulroney's abortion Bill C-43.

It is possible therefore that Magnet's mistaken interpretation of the Charter was due to his failure to understand the powerful weapon that the Charter was placing in the hands of the nine appointed members of the Supreme Court which could and would tie the hands of Parliament by its interpretation of the vague wording of the Charter. They would do so by interpreting the rights in the Charter as having basic guidelines that would limit or restrict rights passed by Parliament. That is, under the Charter the courts could correct Parliament instead of Parliament correcting the courts on rights. Unfortunately, the courts had the final word on rights under the Charter.

In short, Magnet, along with many others, did not foresee that the Supreme Court also could and would wield the Charter as a bludgeon to eliminate traditional values in Canada by declaring some laws as being unconstitutional, not only in regard to abortion, but also on the issues of physician-assisted suicide, prostitution, traditional marriage, medical marijuana and drug-injection sites, religious rights, etc., to name a few of the values tossed aside by the Court in subsequent years. Perhaps, too, as an apparent supporter of the Liberal party, Magnet was prepared to accept the interpretation of the Charter on the abortion issue put forward by the Liberal government. Certainly, his legal opinion coincided precisely with that of the lawyers of the Justice Department.

The legal analysis by Magnet proved fatal to the right to life of the unborn child, since his interpretation became the policy of the CCCB during the negotiations for the Charter and resulted in the CCCB failing to oppose the Charter. Magnet's opinion, of course, was enthusiastically used by both Trudeau and his Justice Minister Chrétien to promote the Charter.

The reason the CCCB did not appear before the Committee was that the Quebec Catholic hierarchy supported the entrenchment of bilingualism in the Charter of Rights, but the bishops from western Canada did not believe, as spiritual leaders of Canada's Catholics, that they should take a position on such a divisive, secular matter. This disagreement led to the failure of the CCCB to present its brief to the Joint Committee of the Senate and House of Commons on the Constitution.

Submission by the Ontario Conference of Catholic Bishops

To ensure some input from the Catholic Church on the Charter, the Ontario Conference of Catholic Bishops stepped in to fill the void. In its brief to the Special Joint Committee on Dec 22, 1980, the Ontario Conference of Catholic Bishops stated:

"The Ontario Conference of Catholic Bishops believes that section 7 as it stands is incomplete and does not sufficiently guarantee the right to life of the unborn child from the moment of conception onward. Therefore the Conference recommends the following rewording:

Everyone from the moment of conception onward until natural death has the right to life. Everyone too, innocent of crime, has the right to liberty and security of the person and the right not to be deprived thereof except in accordance with the principles of fundamental justice."

The brief also supported the position of Campaign Life, "in regard to this organization's position on the rights of the unborn child".[31]

Campaign Life presentation to Special Joint Committee

The desire of the Joint Committee of the Senate and House of Commons on the Constitution to keep the public from understanding the implication of the proposed Charter – namely, that it would undermine Parliamentary supremacy, may have been behind its adamant refusal to permit Campaign Life, the political arm of the pro-life movement from appearing before the Committee. The Liberal members of the Committee were well aware that the impact of a Charter on the abortion law was a matter of concern to a number of Liberal and Progressive Conservative MP's - a concern which the Committee did not want disclosed. Also Campaign Life had been very public in its concerns about the transfer of power from Parliament to the courts. This was a fact that the Committee had not wanted disclosed either.

Nonetheless, some MPs supported the right of Campaign Life to speak before a reluctant Joint Committee on the Constitution.

John Munro (L, Hamilton) wrote to Kathleen Toth on Nov 3, 1980, recommending that her group make representations to the Joint Committee to consider the constitutional proposals, particularly as they contain a charter of rights, one of which is the right to life. [32]

Toth then requested this on November 8 but was flatly refused. She then wrote to all the MPs asking for support. She said she was going to attend anyway.

On November 21, 1980, Perrin Beatty, (PC Wellington Dufferin Simcoe) informed Kathleen Toth that he supported the appearance of Campaign Life before the committee. [33]

On January 8, 1981 four representatives from Campaign Life attended the Joint Committee's session. The delegation consisted of Kathleen Toth, President of Campaign Life, Gwendolyn Landolt, legal counsel for Campaign Life, the main spokesperson, and psychiatrists, Dr. Edward Rzadki and Dr. Michael Barry.

When it was decided that Campaign Life would, in fact, be permitted to testify since it was already present, NDP MP Lorne Nystrom dramatically stood up to show his objection to the presence of the pro-life group, and strode angrily to the back of the room while Campaign Life spoke. He returned to his seat only when Campaign Life's presentation had been completed. Mr. Nystrom threatened to sue Campaign Life if it made public his rude behaviour. Upon being informed that a video was available verifying his behaviour, Mr. Nystrom withdrew his threat.

Toth gave an opening statement to the Committee, then Landolt read the brief.

Toth stated:

"If we do not get legal rights in the constitution for our unborn children – and we have not been able to get the law changed and there is still federal legislation and we have been working very hard; but once it gets into the constitution we will never be able to get it out".

Landolt stated:

"Our concern lies with the proposed entrenched Bill of Rights, which is a sharp departure from the British Parliamentary tradition."

She then noted the apparent lack of interest by Canadians:

"There would appear to be a somewhat curious inertia on the part of many Canadians in respect to the proposed entrenched Charter of Rights. We would suggest a possible explanation for this is the fact that many Canadians are simply not aware of the tremendous implications an entrenched Charter will have on all our lives".

She identified the dangers of the transfer of power to the courts:

"The most important effect of an entrenched Charter of Rights would be that it would give rise to a shift of power from Parliament, which is subject to public opinion, to the Supreme Court of Canada, which is not. This shift in power would then open the door to a wide list of areas in which, for the first time, the judiciary, rather than the legislature, will have the final say."

She cited the U.S. where the charter included the "right to life", which the Supreme Court then ruled excluded the unborn child; "freedom of religion", which the Supreme Court interpreted to exclude the Lord's Prayer in public schools and "freedom of expression", which the Supreme Court has used to strike down state obscenity laws.

She noted the dangers of transferring final powers to the Supreme

Court:

> "The Supreme Court's decision may well not reflect public opinion."

> "The decisions of the Supreme Court may well reflect the views of the nine individuals in the Court rather than that of the general public, which will be permanently and deeply affected by the court's decisions".

She considered it an anachronism to give the courts this power:

> "It would appear essentially undemocratic and an apparent anachronism that judges, who are appointed by the executive, who are not responsible to the people, and who are protected from removal by tenure, be given this tremendous power to impose their will on the elected members of parliament. The rebellion of 1838 in Upper and Lower Canada was undertaken by people determined to end the holding of power by a small group of people. Now we are handing back that power to a small group of people. The Supreme Court will have the power to undermine the will of the people on abortion and other matters. This is "retrogressive and undemocratic". It will be easy to pack the Supreme Court as there are no controls whatever to appointment."

She said in summary on the court issue:

> "It is our view that many of the difficulties and problems that would arise in Canada with an entrenched bill of rights, in our view, the bill of rights should not be entrenched in our constitution...

> Section 1 is a disaster as it allows the court to override everything else in the charter. She recommended it be removed...

> Section 7 should be changed to state that "right to life" shall include "the right to life of the unborn child, conceived but not yet born." Landolt noted that the Advisory Council on the Status of Women wanted "person" used as it would exclude the unborn."

Perrin Beatty then asked Landolt what sections the court would use to strike down any abortion law. Landolt answered that sections 7 and 15 would be likely, to do so. This proved to be accurate as these were the precise sections the Supreme Court used to strike down the abortion law in January 1989.[34]

At the end of Mrs. Landolt's testimony, a senior member of the Committee, Senator Hugette Lapointe stated she was offended by the presentation made by Campaign Life because her deceased father had been a judge, and he would never be biased or unfair in his judgments. Her comment made obvious the fact that the Senator did not grasp the full implications of an entrenched Charter in a Constitution. She was not alone in her misunderstanding of the situation.

Canadians for One Canada submits brief to the Special Joint Committee

James Richardson, national Chairman, Canadians for One Canada, presented his brief to the Special Joint Committee on Dec 16, 1980. Richardson had resigned from the Liberal cabinet in disagreement with Trudeau's plans for the constitution. He rejected the many changes proposed, especially language rights and the transfer of power to the courts.

> *"Our tradition as Canadians has taught us to believe in the supremacy of democratically elected Parliaments and Legislatures and not in the supremacy of written Constitutions...*
>
> *Parliament responds to social and political realities. Courts that interpret a constitution must look at what it says. The country is now much more deeply divided than when the constitutional process began".*

He quoted Trudeau's reasons for the, Charter of Rights given at a speech in Quebec City, Oct 22, 1980:

> *"I'll tell you something else; we also wanted to entrench language rights; unfortunately, I think it's true that, if we had done so, we would have seen certain people in the country fighting the project saying, 'there goes that French power government again, which only wants to help and protect Francophones'. It was to broaden the debate that we wanted to entrench fundamental rights.*
>
> *We knew that neither Mr. Lévesque nor Mr. Ryan would oppose the substance of the move, and they didn't, and that the other provinces would be more likely to support the substance of bilingualism if they had fundamental rights protecting them in the fields of non-discrimination, democratic*

liberties and so on. That was our thinking on the subject."

He closed by asking that Section 16(1), language rights, not be entrenched in the constitution.[35]

Richardson's speech gave the key to understanding why an expanded Charter of Rights was included in the constitution. The quote from Trudeau's speech in Quebec City on October 22 revealed the true reason for the expanded Charter of Rights, which was to obtain approval from the provinces for the Charter, which he would not have obtained if it covered only language rights.

Politicians support the Pro-life side

In Parliament, pro-life MPs continued to demand a better deal for the unborn.

In the House of Commons Debates, Thursday October 23, 1980, Don Mazankowski (PC, Vegreville) asked:

"What about the right to life? That certainly should be basic and fundamental to a charter of human rights. Surely the right to life is a primary and, basic human right on which all other rights depend. Without this right we can have no others, for a human being deprived of his life is deprived forever of all his other rights. The first duty of the state must therefore be the protection of human life, a duty which it owes to every human being before all else. Surely recognition of this, if Parliament is serious about preserving basic human rights, should involve immediately steps to end the legalized murder of unborn children in this country, about 60,000 of them annually." [36]

Pro-abortionists demand the blocking of fetal rights and extension of minority rights

In an article in the *National Catholic Reporter*, an American liberal Catholic newspaper, it was noted regarding the Charter:

"When Doris Anderson was asked by the press in November 1980 why she was requesting a change for the word 'everyone' to 'every person', her answer was 'to exclude the possibility that courts may uphold the rights of fetuses.'" [37]

Gordon Fairweather, chairman of the Human Rights Commission, criticized the new Charter, stating:

"...the proposed charter does not offer sufficient protection against discrimination to women, the disabled, homosexuals and ethnic groups."

He was concerned that it was written in "dangerously broad language which would do little to prevent abuse". He specifically noted:

"...a provision in the charter limiting all rights to 'generally accepted' principles is so 'dangerously broad' that it jeopardizes even such basic rights as protection against discrimination according to race, sex, age and religion."

Continuing, he noted:

"That the anti-discrimination clause in the charter prohibits all types of discrimination in one blanket statement. Failing that, the commission urges the government to add to its list of forbidden grounds for discrimination: physical and mental handicap, marital status, sexual orientation and political belief. (The list already includes race, national origin, colour, religion, age and sex.)"

He ended by asking that the charter be corrected before the constitution was brought home to Canada.[38]

Opposition in the British Parliament came from members worried that Trudeau wanted changes that he had no electoral right to push, and that he was trying to create a republic. Others wanted a consensus in Canada and to clear the proposals in the courts.

In Canada, the western provinces continued to be fiercely opposed to the constitution. In Quebec, Claude Ryan, leader of the provincial Liberal party:

"...urged the federal Government to drop the proposed charter of rights and to bring the constitution to Canada without the proposal for a permanent referendum to resolve constitutional disagreements." [39]

Chrétien responds with pro-abortion amendment S.15 (1) on Jan 9, 1981

One day after the Campaign Life brief was presented to the Joint Committee, Jean Chrétien proposed a change in Section 15(1) as follows:

"Every individual is equal before and under the law and has

a right to the equal protection and equal benefit of the law without discrimination and in particular without discrimination based on race, national or ethnic origin, colour, religion, sex or age."

This was immediately denounced by Campaign Life in a news release January 9, 1981 since the amendment created the possibility of abortion clinics based on the argument that there must be equal access to abortion services. On Jan 19, 1981, it then issued an urgent newsletter on "The life of the unborn child, the charter of rights and abortion clinics".

It noted that the charter as proposed has "placed the life of our unborn children in jeopardy". Also, "it has given rise to a real possibility that abortion clinics will be established in Canada". It continued on to say:

"Chrétien's change to S.15 was:

Original S.15 (1) "Everyone has the right to equality before the law and to the equal protection of the law without discrimination because of race, national or ethnic origin, colour, religion, age or sex."

To S.15(1) " Every individual is equal before and under the law and has the right to the equal protection and equal benefit of the law without discrimination and in particular without discrimination based on race, national or ethnic origin, colour, religion, age or sex."

Laura McArthur, president of the Toronto Right to Life, quoted Larry Henderson, editor of *The Catholic Register*, on October 18, 1980, who said prohibition against discrimination may require Catholic school boards "to accept a teacher who is not a Catholic or whose lifestyle is not consistent with Catholic morals".

McArthur said there also needed to be revisions to the method of appointing judges to the Supreme Court. Also, she noted that if the Bill of Rights was to be entrenched in the constitution, it must set out in the clearest terms the right to life of the unborn child so the Parliament of Canada:

"...could never at any time pass any law which would diminish the unborn child's right to life in any way, except by amending the constitution".

Otherwise the rights of the unborn child will be under constant attack by pro-abortionists in the courts. She argued:

> *"the present Liberal Government argues that the entrench-ment of the Bill of Rights in the proposed constitution would put 'controls' on Parliament, in that it would then no lon-ger have the power to pass laws which could discriminate against, or infringe upon basic freedoms which have been set out in the proposed Bill of Rights…there would be a shift in power from Parliament… to the Supreme Court of Canada which could then, if so asked, look at any of the laws passed by Parliament, and then have the power to throw out any law, if it believed that it infringed any basic right as set out in the constitution."*

Campaign Life accused Chrétien of completely ignoring the briefs presented by Campaign Life and the Ontario Catholic bish-ops.

It noted why Chrétien made the change he did:

> *"According to a CP report dated November 18, 1980, the purpose of their (Advisory Council on the Status of Women) recommendation was to prevent 'fetuses from having pro-tection from the Charter'. The Council believed this would be accomplished by substituting the word 'everyone' by the word 'person' (which was defined by the US Supreme Court in 1973 to exclude the unborn child) and by the addition of the phrase 'every benefit of the law without discrimination'."*

Chrétien argued that he used "individual" instead of "everyone" to make clear that it referred to "natural" persons only, not corpo-rations.

The newsletter stated they were not sure how the courts would interpret "individual", whether to include or exclude the unborn.

Also, McArthur suspected that court rulings against discrimina-tion might force hospitals to provide abortion. She urged followers not to just stand by, but rather, to "enter into the constitutional debate without delay with all our force and might".

Supporters were urged to push for changes in S.7 and S.15 as follows:

> *"S.7 Everyone from the moment of conception onwards, who*

is innocent of any crime, has the absolute right to life. Everyone has the right to liberty and security of person, and the right not to be deprived thereof, except in accordance with the principles of fundamental justice.

S.15(1) Every individual from the moment of conception onwards is equal before and under the law and has the right to the equal protection and equal benefit of the law without discrimination and in particular without discrimination based on race, national or ethnic origin, color, religion, sex or age."[40]

The Right to Life Association of Toronto and Area did a detailed analysis of the proposed constitution. It summarized government reasons for wanting a bill of rights:

a. *The Federal Government only has the power or jurisdiction to pass statutes dealing with federal matters, and thus the federal bill of rights does not and cannot apply to provincial laws and statutes. In effect, the provinces can legally ignore the provisions of the federal Bill of Rights.*

b. *The federal Bill of Rights is merely another statute passed by the federal Parliament, and the federal Parliament can change it in any way and at any time it so wishes. In short, the Bill of Rights is not necessarily permanent, but rather is subject to change at the whim of Parliament. An entrenched Bill of Rights could not be changed by Parliament.*

c. *In the past, when the Bill of Rights has been argued before the Supreme Court, the latter has interpreted it so narrowly and conservatively that it has in actual practice given very little protection to individuals.*

An entrenched Bill of Rights "would put 'controls' on Parliament". Power would shift from Parliament to the courts. [41]

On Friday, Jan 9, 1981 the Joint Senate-House of Commons Constitutional Committee held its last meeting and tabled its report.

Landolt and others distributed a press release denouncing the increased powers of the courts. Landolt wrote to all three major Toronto papers, *The Globe & Mail*, *Toronto Sun* and *Toronto Star*, on January 12, 1981, lamenting "the curious inertia on the part of many Canadians in respect to the proposed entrenched Charter of Rights". She then went on to say:

> "To put it in a historical perspective it seems that the transfer of final power from Parliament which is sensitive to public opinion to the few individuals on the Supreme Court of Canada who are not sensitive to public opinion, which would be the result of an entrenched charter, is contrary to the principles fought so hard for in the Rebellions of Upper and Lower Canada just over one hundred years ago. Certainly one of the reasons for the rebellions was the objection to a handful of individuals appointed by the government having the final say on the pressing social and political issues of the day. This would occur in Canada again if the entrenched Charter of Rights is endorsed." [42]

In a letter to Jean Chrétien on January 28, 1981, Landolt warned him about the implications of his changes to s.15 and their effects on abortion.

> "The whole effect of s.15 will depend upon how the Supreme Court of Canada interprets the word "individual" (or "everyone" for that matter). If the Court interprets "individual" or "everyone" so as to exclude the unborn, then s.15 would be used by the pro-abortionists to argue before the courts that women are being discriminated against in any of those localities where hospitals do not provide abortions and that they are thereby being denied equal access to the alleged "benefit" of the [abortion] law.
>
> It is important to note that under another amendment to the Charter proposed by you on January 12, 1981, the Court will be empowered to apply the "remedies" as it considers "just and appropriate". Thus, if the Court determines that there is discrimination under s.15, it could order a certain hospital to provide abortions, or, it could even go further by ordering the provincial Minister of Health to widen the access to abortion by requiring him to "approve" more hospitals for abortion. Quite literally hundreds and thousands of lives will depend upon this proposed amendment to s.15 (1) of the Charter. I am wondering, therefore, whether it was the intention of your government that this amendment would have such a direct effect on the abortion issue in Canada?" [43]

The arguments outlined by Landolt above were in fact some of the very arguments applied by the Supreme Court in striking down the abortion law.

On January 28, 1981 Landolt wrote to many senators and MPs asking them to amend s.15:

> *"It would be deeply appreciated, therefore, if you would endeavour to take steps that are necessary to have s.15 amended so that this section will not be used by the abortionists to widen access to the abortion law as outlined in the memorandum."*

As a result of the correspondence, it can be said that there were few, if any MPs and Senators, who did not know the dangers of transferring control over laws from Parliament to judges and its effects on the abortion issue.

In a news release on March 16, 1981, Landolt, who was also legal counsel for the Right to Life Association of Toronto and Area, provided a perceptive prediction on the future of abortion in Canada. She wrote:

> *"Abortion on demand has been locked into the proposed new Charter of Rights".*

She explained that the Supreme Court of Canada refused to hear an appeal from the Dehler case on abortion in 1979 leaving standing a decision that the unborn child had rights only once it was born. Therefore, s.7 and s.15 will not apply to the unborn child. Moreover s.15 gives women complete and absolute rights. Any restrictions on abortion would be deemed unconstitutional. Our wording in the charter is similar to the US 14th amendment, under which the US Supreme Court found a right to privacy which included a right to abortion.

She then gave an accurate timetable of what would and did happen:

1981 charter of rights passed

1984 s.15 (1) will come into effect

1986-1987 first test cases on abortion will reach the courts

1988-1989 the Supreme Court will hand down its decision in favour of abortion on demand.

She noted, in 1981, that over 100,000 children had been killed in hospitals since Trudeau passed the abortion law in 1969. (44) Moreover, hospitals themselves stopped publishing the number of abortions they committed making it impossible to get accurate statistics from them.

A final note on the power of politicians and judges was given by Plamondon who wrote:

> *"The courts furnished another popular haven for Liberal ministers. While the Canadian Bar Association generally approved of Trudeau's appointments to the Supreme Court, they expressed concern about how he treated lower-court appointments. After Trudeau arranged for three federal court appointments on his retirement, the Bar Association wrote, 'At present, the [federal] Court is perceived by many, rightly or wrongly, as a government-oriented court because so many former politicians and federal officials have been appointed to it...As to appointments to the Federal Court of Canada, political favouritism has been a dominant, though not sole, consideration. Many appointees have been active supporters of the party in power.'"* [45]

Chapter 5

Concerns about transfer of power to nine unelected judges

UK concerns about a charter of rights

The UK had come under pressure from the European Union to implement a charter of rights. This occurred after Westminster ratified the European Convention on Human Rights, which dispositions had not been incorporated into English law at the time that Trudeau came asking for a constitution with a charter of rights for Canada. The British Prime Minister Margaret Thatcher and many others in her government opposed any charter of rights for the United Kingdom. To them Parliament was supreme. They would not change this. Bastien quotes Lord Diplock, one of the Law Lords (the equivalent of Supreme Court judges in Canada), warning:

> *"It seems to me that those who represent the people have been elected democratically in representative parliament know better and are better judges than appointed judges, who have been appointed not for their social philosophies or their politics but because of their qualification in the law. If this bill (EU Convention) becomes law in its present form, it will be open to every fanatic, every crackpot, to challenge any law they disagree with."* [1]

Journalists, judges and lawyers opposed the transfer

Not only pro-life groups in Canada were concerned with passing control to judges. Members of the judiciary themselves also expressed concerns. Journalist Robert Sheppard, in an article entitled "Supreme Court wary of entrenched bill of rights", July 30, 1980, in *The Globe and Mail*, noted some warnings made about the Charter by judges. He wrote:

> *"When the Supreme Court of Canada returns in October... it may find itself with important new powers that are only dimly perceived but could drastically change the face of Canadian federalism.*
>
> *If the first ministers agree in September to entrench a bill of rights in the Constitution, then the Supreme Court would become more like its U.S. counterpart. For the first time in parliamentary history, it will be able to impose its will on elected members and act as a check on the power of the majority...*
>
> *These far reaching powers would probably first be felt in the field of minority-language rights. However, the process opens the door to a wide list of areas in which the judiciary rather than the politicians could have the final say: Are discriminatory work laws or affirmative-action programs constitutional? Does abortion violate the pursuit of life and liberty? Is provincial censorship of movies against freedom of speech?"*

He went on to note that Louis-Philippe Pigeon, a member of the Supreme Court (1967-1983) warned that:

> *"it would mean a significant shift of power to the court with a lack of awareness of the consequences. A constitutional bill of rights means a delegation of legislative power to a court to an extent that is undefinable. It doesn't matter how it is worded, the actual extent will be what the court says it is."*

Sheppard wrote that Professor Schmeiser, a constitutional expert from the University of Saskatchewan, was one of many who argued against the entrenchment of a bill of rights on the grounds that it would benefit only lawyers and create unnecessary litigation, and that the courts are not the best-equipped institutions to deal with what are essentially political problems. Schmeiser had stated in his submission to the Joint Committee that there is an:

"...essentially undemocratic aspect of judicial review" given that judges are appointed and are protected from removal by tenure. It is a worrying prospect that five old men, a bare majority on the Supreme Court, could rule on the great social and political issues of the nation contrary to and regardless of the wishes of the populace."

Schmeiser noted numerous other concerns including: lessening of prestige of the Supreme Court as it became embroiled in blatantly political decisions; the clogging of the system by well-organized lobby groups which could afford litigation; the creation of false hopes because of the confusion that might follow; the lack of prescribed procedures; and, finally, the entrenched bill of rights in the U.S. had created a tendency towards uniformity and centralization of authority and power in that country, trends that are out of keeping with those of a federal state like Canada.

Sheppard continued in his article:

"One cannot help but wonder how such provincial legislative schemes as compulsory automobile insurance, universal hospitalization, and Medicare would have fared under judicial review".

Sheppard then quoted Mr. Justice Ronald Martland, another member of the Supreme Court of Canada (1958 to 1982) who also expressed warnings about the power of the courts under the charter:

"Who would really support the setting up of a Charter of Rights.

It is very difficult to define rights in specific terms, and that is where the problems arise for the courts. A generalized phrase has to be spelled out in particular circumstances, and that means you are transferring enormous amounts of power to the tribunal. As a charter of rights is pretty well written in stone, it is the court that has to spell out the consequences and, in turn, those become precedents for use in later cases. As for the protection of citizens, the Soviet Union has 'one of the broadest charters of civil rights' in the world, but 'we all know how that has worked out'."

Sheppard ended the article by noting that Roy Romanow, the Saskatchewan Intergovernmental Affairs Minister who was co-chairman of the constitutional talks, was worried that the federal government might move to enact a charter of rights unilaterally, seeing it as a popular symbolic issue.

Among lawyers to speak out against the transfer of power was Philip Jeffrey Traversy, LLP. In his comments, included in an ad by Campaign Life in the *Toronto Star* on March 26, 1981, Mr. Traversy said that all the interpretations by Campaign Life were possible. "The only control on the Supreme Court is its own sense of self-restraint". In the US courts disregard the original intention of the framers of the Constitution.

"Few understand how much of a gamble a Charter of Rights can be".

He worried about the powers of the Supreme Court.

"Such judicial decisions can only be overruled by constitutional amendment (very difficult) or by replacing the judges (very difficult)."

He suggested a woman would easily get the court to approve an abortion. He stated:

"A Charter of Rights has inherent in it the possibility of important and unwanted changes in our society's values being imposed on us".

He noted that in the US activists and lawyers work tirelessly to overturn laws often totally contrary to the original Bill of Rights. He closed by saying:

"Without clear and specific amendments to cover the points raised by Campaign Life, this Charter should not be passed."

A copy of his letter was sent to all Liberal MPs.

Media worried about judges

Even the *Toronto Star*, normally totally supportive of all Liberal actions, complained about the erosion of the supremacy of Parliament. Marvin Lipton, writing in the *Toronto Star*, January 19, 1981, stated:

"Changes announced last week in the federal government's proposed constitutional charter of rights would destroy the

supremacy of Parliament by giving the courts much greater power to interpret and override legislative acts."

In an editorial in the *Windsor Star* on November 6, 1980, Dick Spicer, in an article entitled "The Charter of Rights What it means to Canadians", stated the Charter of Rights would bring sweeping changes to our way of life and gave as examples, the ending of Sunday store closings, and the removal of a right to censor movies. The Supreme Court would assume a more active role in questioning Canadian laws.

Spicer noted that this new charter would allow the Supreme Court to nullify laws. With new appointments, the majority of the court could move from a conservative to a liberal stance. This, of course, is exactly what occurred.

The *Toronto Sun* was a strong opponent of the constitutional proposal with a charter of rights. In an article on November 20, 1980, Peter Worthington referred to a paper by G.P. Browne, a history professor at Carleton, which argued against entrenching a bill of rights into the constitution. Browne had stated:

"What 'entrenching' a Bill of Rights in our constitution means is that the Supreme Court would have authority to disallow laws passed by the federal and provincial governments on the grounds that these laws contravene 'fundamental' rights. At the moment the Supreme Court does not have this authority, but it would have it in future.

This means that the role of the Supreme Court would be changed to become responsible for defining basic social values. In other words legislative authority that presently resides with elected and accountable representatives would be transferred to appointed and tenured judges."

Rather than enhance and protect rights and liberties, such a move could restrict and threaten them. Anyone who believes that parliamentary democracy, despite its flaws, is the best form of government for Canada, should immediately be alarmed at this development. It amounts to a "constitutional revolution" entailing the relinquishment of the essential principle of Parliamentary democracy – that parliament is supreme."

Worthington continued:

"Putting a bill of rights into the constitution also marks a 'shift' away from the British system to the American system. While both are 'representative democracies', with governmental power exercised by the 'people' through their elected representatives, and both systems seek to protect minorities and individuals against governmental discriminations, the methods used to achieve this protection are quite different."

"Those who believe that "entrenching" the Bill of Rights into the constitution is the best way to protect rights and liberties (Trudeau and Davis), overlook the reality that some of the vilest dictatorships boast the most elaborate and all-inclusive bill of rights, which are often "entrenched".

"A simple example like the right to life changes with the times and has various interpretations with regards to abortion, capital punishment, euthanasia, etc. In short, the more general and qualified a bill of rights is, the more room it allows for interpretation and the more power it gives to whoever interprets it. Entrenchment is a trap. Also, if Canada let judges interpret the law, whoever appoints judges becomes very powerful. In Canada, the Prime Minister alone has this power if he chooses to wield it."

Worthington closed by saying:

"Canadians cannot be too cautious about any changes that would appreciably increase the legislative authority of the judiciary and decrease that of federal and provincial parliaments.

But after reading this, does Bill Davis or anyone truly think "entrenching" a Bill of Rights in the constitution guarantees or protects anything? How can he, or anyone?"

In a *Toronto Star* article, "A tough, new role faces Supreme Court", published on December 26, 1980, Chief Justice Bora Laskin was referred to as being appalled by the notion that a court could be biased. The article quoted Laskin:

"Our duty as a judge is to the law and the impartial administration of justice", says Chief Justice Bora Laskin. He is appalled by suggestions that the court tilts one way or another.

"Do we lean? Of course we do – in the direction in which the

*command of the constitution take us according to our indi-
vidual understandings."*

Among the changes identified in the article, the first was that
judges might start allowing data that covered every conceivable
aspect of an issue.

Another article in the same paper on the same day, entitled "9
Aloof Men Who Shy Away from Publicity", identified two judges
who would have increased powers:

*"Julien Chouinard, 51, is one of a fine line of brilliant lawyers
to come from Quebec. A Rhodes scholar, he was appointed
last year by former Prime Minister Joe Clark. Chouinard
comes with credentials as a tough, strict, yet modern jurist
who earned bravos for his stints as deputy minister of justice
for Quebec and later on the Quebec Court of Appeal.*

*Although by reputation a conservative – he ran for the federal
Tories in 1958 – Chouinard was successful in bringing down
a fair, widely acclaimed report on the volatile bilingual air
traffic control issue...*

*"Antonio Lamer, 47, is the youngest member of the bench
and is still finding his feet after his appointment last March.*

*Born in Montreal, he describes himself as a 'state employed
activist' and once criticized the Supreme Court for not
protecting individual liberties."*

Writing the article "Rights Charter Boosts Court's Power" in *The
Globe and Mail*, January 13th, 1981, Robert Sheppard acknowledged that the Liberals knew changes were required in order to
have legislation passed.

*"The changes, set out by Justice Minister Jean Chrétien last
night before the special parliamentary committee on the
constitution, are designed to salvage the Government's heavily criticized reform package before it is sent to the British
Parliament for amendment and patriation."*

The changes included:

*"...several new sections on language, legal and native rights,
as well as a broad new 'remedies clause', which will allow
the courts to order compensation or remedial action in cases
where rights have been violated."*

It is noteworthy that French language rights in Ontario were not added to the charter due to opposition from Ontario Premier Bill Davis.

Politicians worried about the power of the courts

Premier Brian Peckford of Newfoundland stated that prohibition against discrimination may eliminate religious (denominational) schools in that province. [2]

Horace Carver, Justice Minister for PEI, opposed giving the courts more power.

> *"If the intention is to give more power to the courts, this province would not only be in opposition, but would seriously question what type of society, what system of governing, we would have."* [3]

Various MPs also spoke out about the power of the courts under the charter. For example, in a debate on capital punishment and abortion on March 5, 1981, Stan Darling (PC, Parry Sound-Muskoka) gave a remarkably accurate analogy of exactly what would occur under an entrenched charter of rights. He said that there were:

> *"...two issues the fate of which must be decided by the people through their elected representatives. They are moral issues which cannot, and must not, be decided by the courts. By shifting the responsibility to the courts, this government seeks to avoid dealing with matters under its jurisdiction and deprives the people of Canada of a voice in the forum of debate."* [4]

Among those in the Senate to warn about transferring power to the courts was Senator Eric Cook. He spoke out against transferring control from Parliament to the courts with the Charter of Rights, and referenced the court decision in 1928 that said "persons" did not include women. He suggested different ways of entrenching a charter. His preference was for one that:

> *"...even if the Supreme Court were to declare a law contrary to the Charter, that law could still be passed, providing certain requirements were met." He called this a Charter of Rights with 'priority status'."*

He then gave another powerful quote from Professor Browne,

Professor of History at Carleton University:

> *"Are they (who support Charter) really willing to allow our basic moral values to be ultimately defined, not by our elected and accountable representatives, but by nine appointed judges – who are largely chosen by the federal government, if not the prime minister, and who are not, like their American counterparts, subject to the scrutiny and approval of an elected body representing both the people and the provinces? Are they also prepared to chance the possible consequences of such an extreme transfer of legislative responsibility – a further politicizing of the supreme court, an increasing doubt as to the impartiality of our judges, a diminution of confidence in our legal system, a decreased respect for the Rule of Law, a reduced role for our elected representatives, an inferior status for our parliaments, a dwindling participation in the political process, and the effects of all these changes on our sense of community, not to speak of national unity?"* [5]

Chapter 6

Cardinal Carter supports the Charter of Rights

Pro-lifers look to the Catholic Church for leadership

As the battle raged against Trudeau's constitutional proposals, many people in the pro-life movement looked to the Catholic Church for leadership. Jim Hughes, president of Campaign Life, recalls that Pope John Paul II was so strong that most thought the Canadian bishops would be likewise. They believed that all other denominations would look to the Catholics and follow its lead. Jim noted that people trusted the Catholic Church. Unfortunately, many in the church hierarchy thought the pro-life activists were radicals, or, more appropriately, reactionary. Jim Hughes and others soon came to realize that the church was weak in its resolve to uphold moral values. The *Winnipeg Statement* on birth control in 1968 and other changes had sapped resistance. Even so, Campaign Life still persisted in seeking support from the Catholic bishops to raise objections to the charter.[1]

Pro-life groups not funded were always short of funds, not being supported by Liberal government largesse as the pro-abortion, feminist and other radical groups were.

Consequently, Campaign Life made appeals to the bishops for money from time to time.

The Ontario Conference of Catholic Bishops showed interest in supporting the pro-life cause but backed off at times because of divisions they saw within the pro-life groups. In one instance, Fr. A.J. Macdougall, SJ, the General Secretary of the Ontario Conference of Catholic Bishops, in a letter, dated June 27, 1978, wrote to Paul Formby, National coordinator of Campaign Life stating:

"At a recent executive meeting of the Ontario Conference of Catholic bishops, June 21, there was a thorough discussion of the pro-life situation in Ontario. Involved was the question of financial support by the Ontario bishops of Alliance for Life, Coalition for Life and Campaign Life.

If the Ontario bishops have any outstanding commitment of support, it is to Coalition for Life because of an agreement made between it and Alliance for Life in 1976 and later communicated to the bishops.

However, at the present time, the bishops are withholding all financial assistance to the three pro-life groups until some kind of reconciliation and united stand can be achieved. They specifically ask that representatives of the three organizations get together and work out some suitable arrangement that all could agree to. The organizations then could inform the bishops of any common policy.

The bishops want to be fair to all concerned, but they are apprehensive about the current divisiveness and disarray affecting the pro-life movement in Ontario. They must rely on the goodwill of the pro-life organizations themselves to sort out the present difficulties and create a more harmonious approach." [2]

Another appeal by Campaign Life in late 1980 led to outright rejection. Fr. Patrick Kennedy, Assistant General Secretary of the CCCB explained on Dec 3, 1980:

"Although the CCCB is not a funding organization, the CCCB does provide some funding for the educational arm of the pro-life movement that is Alliance. The monies provided to the pro-life group mentioned do not originate with this

conference but are given to it for this purpose from other sources.

Perhaps you could more effectively appeal at the diocesan level. Although they too are under the same restrictions regarding the funding of any non-registered organization." [3]

Jim Hughes remembered another occasion when Campaign Life asked if they could receive funding from the Share Life funds. They were told, no way. [4]

The bishops however did seek to better understand the pro-life groups. On Dec 18, 1980, Fr. Patrick Kennedy, Assistant General Secretary of the CCCB, wrote to Kathleen Toth asking for details on the founding, membership and financial status of Campaign Life. [5]

Cardinal Carter appointed Father Brad Massman, responsible for public relations for the Toronto Catholic Archdiocese, to represent him in a meeting with Hughes, saying he would join in "if some fruitful arrangement and dialogue can be initiated on this level."[6] Nothing came of this.

On January 27, 1981 an appeal letter was sent by Campaign Life to the bishops asking them to oppose the Charter. It pointed out the deception of the Charter:

"The Charter and its amendments are a masterpiece of deception because the intent is not precise and the wording is deliberately vague and open to broad interpretations by the judiciary. The Charter attempts to be totally neutral. Experience has shown that the position of neutrality will amount to nothing less than the sudden replacement of the Christian morality with the entrenchment of the modern hedonist morality and its corrupting influence."

It noted key flaws in the Charter:

"The following are totally ignored and, or denied:

a. *The "Principles of Fundamental Justice" referred to in the Charter do not state that they are based on the traditional Judeo-Christian ethic. There is no definition given and God is totally ignored.*

b. *The right to life should be listed as a fundamental right and not a legal right and the wording of this section de-*

liberately ignores the preborn, the handicapped and the aged whose lives are in today's world being taken and continually threatened by liberal legislation.

c. *The family unit is not mentioned in the Charter and given certain rights which should supersede many individual rights.*

d. *Our separate schools in several provinces are not given the right and protection required to guarantee their future rights to exist, to expand, or to function according to our traditions. They are subject to individual rights."*

The letter then asked all bishops to use their "maximum personal influence on the politicians who represent their diocese."[7] An identical letter was sent to leaders of other faiths, and to all the members of Parliament. This warning was disregarded.

As the Liberal government changed aspects of the Charter, pro-life groups alerted the bishops to keep them well informed. For example, on February 10, 1981, Landolt wrote to key members of the hierarchy, including Cardinal Carter and Archbishop MacNeil, President of the Canadian Conference of Catholic Bishops, warning them of the dangers of Chrétien's amendment to section 15(1):

"There are two extremely important effects to this amendment of s.15 in that it will mean:

1. *The enshrinement into the Canadian constitution of the equivalent of the highly controversial US Equal Rights Amendment (ERA): in fact, the language of the proposed Canadian amendment is much stronger than that of the American amendment;*

2. *Lead to the establishment of abortion clinics, or at the very least, a greatly increased number of hospitals being required to provide abortion services. It will also lead to a constitutionally based right to government funded abortions."*

She also noted it would undermine the family and force provinces to provide abortions. [8]

She also wrote to supportive leaders of other faiths, such as the Rev. R.W. Taitinger, General Superintendent of the Pentecostal Assemblies.

This letter of warning was also sent to all MPs.

Cardinal Carter supports the Charter

During the charter debate, according to MP Garnet Bloomfield (Liberal, London/Middlesex), Trudeau advised his caucus that he was concerned about the growing impact of the pro-life movement to resist an entrenched Charter of Rights because it would be detrimental to the abortion issue. Trudeau referred to the pro-life resistance having started only as a small cloud on the horizon, but that it was growing significantly each day, so that it may well prevent the Charter's passage, if its influence was not stopped.

Trudeau had a solution to this problem: namely, the impact of the pro-life movement could be broken if Cardinal Carter, Archbishop of Toronto, would be persuaded to come onside, to support the Charter. This way, Trudeau reasoned the consciences of Catholic and other faith-based MPs, could be freed to vote for the Charter. Each weekly caucus day, Trudeau would update his MPs on the progress he was making in his negotiations with Cardinal Carter.

Toronto lawyer John Stephens and Gwen Landolt, legal counsel for Campaign Life, met with the pro-life caucus in February 1981 and warned them of the impact of the charter on the abortion issue. Mrs. Ursula Appolloni, (L, York South/Weston) attended that meeting.

MP Ursula Appolloni was well known as a pro-life Liberal MP. For example, she was the MP who, in 1975, presented the million pro-life signatures to Parliament. She was prominent in the Liberal party and wrote a weekly article in the *Catholic Register*. Her role in the Charter debate was to assure that pro-life MPs did not stray from the Liberal resolution on the constitution. It was surprising that she accepted this assignment. Perhaps she agreed to this to advance her own political career. It's possible, however, that she may have genuinely trusted and believed Trudeau's views on the issue, backed by the opinion of the Justice Department.

MP Appolloni's hercularian efforts on behalf of the Liberal party to ensure all Liberal MPs supported the government's constitutional resolution, did not advance her career, except that she did serve as Parliamentary Secretary to the Minister of National Defense from 1980 to 1982. Mrs. Appolloni did not run in the 1984 federal election. She was not given a patronage appointment, often awarded to former MPs in appreciation for the services to the party due to changing political circumstances. Trudeau had resigned as party leader in February 1984, and the new Liberal leader, John Turner, elected in June, 1984. Turner did not owe any debt to Mrs. Appolloni. Further, there was little time for the Liberal party to make any appointments since it was shortly defeated by the Progressive Conservative leader, Brian Mulroney in the September 1984 federal election. The world had moved on.

After the pro-life caucus meeting, Mrs. Appolloni issued the first blast from her shotgun in a letter dated February 13, 1981 which she sent to all Liberal MP's. She stated:

"As you probably know, I have long been a vocal advocate of the rights of the unborn. Indeed, for three elections I have staked my reputation on this vital point and, indeed, at one time allowed my career to suffer rather than give up the fight.

I may add that not all the problems I encountered came from pro-abortionists. With all the good will in the world, pro-lifers too, with their rhetoric, frequently caused more harm than good.

The present Constitutional debate is a case in point. One pro-life lawyer (a known Tory sympathizer) says the new Charter will harm the unborn. At least one dozen other lawyers have personally assured me it will not.

I now hear that even Cardinal Carter is satisfied with the new amendment. Under these circumstances, I will vote for the amended Charter in good conscience.

I personally welcome the amendment. Indeed, the use of the word "individual" can only help any lawyer who has to defend an unborn child in court. With the increased knowledge we now have of biology, it would be difficult to prove the baby is not an individual. Thus, the amended clause 15 should certainly help our cause." [9]

Her reference to "at least one dozen lawyers" can only be interpreted to mean the lawyers from the Justice Department - scarcely a reliable source of impartial legal advice, as noted earlier.

By March 1981, individuals and groups were expressing their concerns about Cardinal Carter's position on the Charter. On

March 9, 1981 Earl Amyotte of Campaign Life of Southwestern Ontario wrote the *Windsor Star* stating:

> *"We are mystified as to why the Cardinal has withdrawn his opposition to the Charter. Has not the Roman Catholic Church taken a very positive stance on this issue as evidenced by the quite remarkable statements on abortion by Pope John Paul II? Is it possible that the Cardinal differs with the Pope on the importance of this matter and the necessity to protect the unborn child, or does the Cardinal think there are more important matters at stake here?"*

On March 31, 1981, Ursula Appolloni sent a memorandum to all Liberal MPs stating:

> *"I had a call from the Archdiocese of Toronto this morning, informing me that Cardinal Carter had issued a statement to the Catholic Register to the effect that he is convinced the Charter is neutral on the subject of abortion. He further adds that it is wrong for people to accuse those who support the Charter of immorality inasmuch as the Charter itself entrenches many moral rights. At the same time, however, he is obviously concerned about the abortion laws in Canada.*
>
> *The Canadian Conference of Catholic Bishops retained legal counsel to review the Charter and particularly the opinions given by Mrs. Landolt and Mr. Stephens. I am now informed that this counsel too agrees with the opinion we have already received from the Department of Justice."* [10]

The day Cardinal Carter officially announced his support for the Charter, MP Garnet Bloomfield described the reaction to this by the Liberal caucus:

> *"MP Ursula Appolloni (York South-Weston) entered the lounge behind the House of Commons, waving her hands stating "we're free, we're free, if it's good enough for the Cardinal, it's good enough for me!" And the caucus went wild. MPs hugged each other, jumped on chairs, announcing that the chains that had prevented them from voting for the Charter were now broken. The Liberal MPs had been under a lot of pressure to not support the government bill on the Charter because of concerns about the abortion issue, and they were now free to do so.* [11]

Copies of the Cardinal's statement were widely distributed by the Liberal MPs to their constituents in special mailings to them to justify their party's refusal to entrench a pro-life provision in the Charter.

In any case, despite her endorsement of Cardinal Carter's position on the Charter, Appolloni had her own private doubts on the issue. She wrote to Justice Minister Chrétien seeking assurances that the opinions expressed by the two pro-life lawyers at the pro-life caucus meeting in February were without legal merit.

On April 15, 1981, Mr. Chrétien replied to her in his usual in convoluted style which he assured her that S.7 of the proposed Charter would not allow for abortions. This section of the Charter, of course, was precisely one of the provisions in the Charter which the Supreme Court of Canada applied to strike down the abortion law in the *Morgentaler* case. Mr. Chrétien stated in his letter as follows:

> *"The Canadian Supreme Court has not given the 'due process' clause in the present Bill of Rights (the right not to be deprived of liberty without due process of law) a substantive content, but confined its scope to a requirement of procedural fairness only. Consequently, it has not tested the substantive value or fairness of laws against the 'due process' clause. However, to ensure that the United States approach will never be imported into Canadian law in the future, we have removed the 'due process of law' wording from section 7 and replaced it with the test of 'in accordance with the principles of fundamental justice'. Thus the right to liberty is subject to deprival not in accordance with due process of law but in accordance with the principles of fundamental justice. This wording will make it doubly clear that the right to liberty will not be subject to a substantial fairness test, but only to a procedural fairness test.*

> *Consequently under section 7 of the Charter, a person may always be deprived of his or her liberty (privacy) as long as the law provided for the deprivation is procedurally fair, i.e., by a fairer and impartial hearing, and there will therefore be no constitutionally entrenched right to privacy or abortion."*

Cardinal Carter's support of the Charter had been formally

announced in the *Catholic Register* on April 4, 1981. The article stated:

> *"[Cardinal Carter] strongly reaffirms the necessity of protecting the life of the unborn. He recounts conversations and letters with the Prime Minister and Senior Counsel of the Department of Justice. He proposes amendments which would strengthen the rights of the unborn. What he does not accept, after his conversations and correspondence, is that there is any attempt on the part of the Government or its Constitutional Package to lessen the rights of the unborn or to make abortion on demand available. He is satisfied that this is clearly not the intention of the Government. He does state "I hold the Prime Minister and the Government of Canada accountable for any diminishment to the rights of the unborn which may flow from this Charter.*
>
> *Having decided to take this position based on what the Bishops considered to be the best legal opinion available, and having decided on an appropriate procedure to have the legislators state their intent, the Cardinal is therefore obliged to state that he does not agree with the different legal opinion and the different procedures of Campaign Life.*
>
> *The Cardinal and Bishops of Canada have reiterated that they remain vehemently opposed to any attempt to expand legal avenues which open the way to abortion. The disagreement with Campaign Life is over the interpretation of the intent of the proposed Charter and the method being followed in responding to the Charter."*

In its background paper, the Canadian Conference of Catholic Bishops stated:

> *"Throughout the debate on the proposed Constitution and Charter of Rights, the Canadian Conference of Catholic Bishops has made it clear that Catholics are free to support any political position with respect to the Constitution and Charter of Rights. The Bishops have carefully refrained from supporting any political party, and from taking position on the desirability or political expediency of the Constitutional package. They have constantly sought to deal only with the justice of the proposed Charter and its moral and legal impli-*

cations. They do not oppose the Charter on moral grounds."

At the same time, in order to back Cardinal Carter's position on the charter, Msgr. Dennis Murphy, of the CCCB, on April 6, 1981, sent Kathleen Toth, President of Campaign Life, the legal opinion of Joseph Magnet, Q.C., giving it as the reason why the CCCB supported the Charter. It stated that Parliament can create new rights, such as a right to life for the unborn, by criminalizing abortions, by amending s.251. It also said it was unlikely that the courts would introduce a right to privacy. [12]

Toronto's *Sunday Sun* newspaper columnist, Claire Hoy, on April 5, 1981, in response to Cardinal Carter's statement, wrote:

> *"Even if the Charter doesn't "worsen" the situation – although it likely will, since as Carter admits, it doesn't protect the unborn – the fact is approximately 500,000 abortions have been performed in Canada the last 10 years under current laws.*
>
> *How then can Carter claim a commitment to 'opposing abortion in every possible way' while endorsing a Charter which, at the very least, won't do anything to stop the current flood of abortions?*
>
> *Carter says he's satisfied it won't lead to 'abortion on demand' as some groups claim. Maybe, maybe not. Either way, abortion on demand isn't the issue. Abortion is. Period."*

The Cardinal and the bishops of Canada repeated several times over the next few months that, although they vehemently opposed any attempt to expand legal avenues which opened the way to abortion, they nonetheless, stood by the legal opinion of their lawyer, Joseph Magnet, and were of the view that the Charter would not endanger the life of the unborn child.

Some Catholic bishops also issued separate statements in support of Cardinal Carter's position. They were: Bishop Sherlock of the Diocese of London, Archbishop Gervais of Ottawa and Archbishop Wall of Winnipeg. According to Jim Hughes, the Quebec bishops were only interested in the bilingual question. [13]

If Cardinal Carter, as the most prominent Catholic leader in Canada, thought that his decision on the Charter would settle the matter once and for all, he misread the pro-life movement. It was not just a "Catholic" movement. It had strong Catholics as leaders, for sure, but it also had strong Protestant leaders, as well as a sprinkling of atheists. One didn't have to be "religious" or Catholic to be concerned about the human right to life of unborn children endangered by the Charter.

The struggle for the life of the unborn child continued unabated, despite Cardinal Carter's support of the Charter. The leaders in the pro-life movement continued to lobby against the Charter and to publicly question Cardinal Carter's support of it. It wondered whether the Cardinal believed there were more important matters at stake in the Charter than the necessity to protect the unborn child.

Marie Turcotte, director of the Family Survival Fund, wrote all Canadian bishops on April 17, 1981 saying:

> "Before it is too late and the Charter is passed we beg the bishops of Canada to once again denounce the Charter and repudiate Cardinal Carter's position on behalf of all Canadian Catholics. This would help us recover the ground we lost due to the Cardinal's statements, which incidentally, were also repeated by Liberals in the House of Commons debate. This would put the pressure back on the Liberal pro-life MPs to have the charter properly amended.
>
> Mr. Trudeau has betrayed many of our Christian principles in the 1969 amendment to the Criminal Code. If the Cardinal wants us to trust him then why has Trudeau not taken the simple step of putting it in writing in the constitution while at the same time correct the serious problem he has already created? Mr. Trudeau has already demonstrated over and over again that he is a utilitarian humanist."...
>
> Members of our group have exclaimed "My God, My God, why did the Cardinal forsake us?"

Turcotte said that the Liberal pro-abortionists were laughing at them:

> "Instead of Cardinal Carter persuading Trudeau, it's Trudeau who persuades Carter. Meanwhile Trudeau, Chrétien, Lalonde, Bégin and all the rest of the abortionist leaders now jeer at us and are laughing in their beards at the mass confusion. Meanwhile they are taking this opportunity to press onward full steam before we regroup and the pressure

can be built up again on their wavering backbenchers." [14]

On April 14, 1981, Jan de Villiers, a public servant, wrote Landolt asking her to give a document to Cardinal Carter. The document stated:

> *"What may happen will now be a replay of 1969. Your Church failed once before; will it now fail for the second, and the last time?"*

His document, entitled *"A Last Warning"*, noted that the proposed constitution:

> "May be calculated to:
> a. *Deny the sovereignty of parliament;*
> b. *Extinguish or disable the unwritten parts of the Canadian Constitution;*
> c. *Remove the historical basis upon which the liberties and the fundamental rights of Canadians have rested, and*
> d. *Open the way for further fundamental changes over which neither the people nor the Parliament of Canada may have any control...*
>
> *Not only will the counterbalancing functions of provincially elected legislatures, in such important fields as civil and property rights, be removed, but with the accompanying contraction of the functions of Parliament itself, there may be an inordinate concentration of power in the hands of the Executive, the bureaucracy and the Courts, and with the power of appointment of the judges remaining in the gift of the Executive, as before."* [15]

Letters to the editor in newspapers and to Cardinal Carter personally, continued to criticize him for his support of the Charter.

This criticism and the continuing turmoil over the abortion issue and the Charter, led Cardinal Carter to issue a "clarifying" statement on his position. On April 29, 1981 he placed an advertisement in *The Globe and Mail*, attempting to clarify his position. This clarification extended the support for his position to the Canadian Conference of Catholic bishops as well.

The advertisement read:

> *"In view of the distortion and misrepresentation of my position concerning aspects of the proposed Canadian Charter*

of Rights, I wish to make the following statement for purposes of clarification.

At no time have I "approved" "endorsed" or otherwise offered support to this Charter. At the request of the President of the Canadian Conference of Catholic Bishops, Archbishop Joseph N. MacNeil of Edmonton, I made representation to the Prime Minister on the Church's position re: Catholic education, native rights and the protection of the unborn child. Subsequently I expressed myself as satisfied with assurances I received on the first two subjects but dissatisfied with the Charter's failure to protect human life from the beginning. My request for an amendment to Sections 15 or 7 was not met. I continue to regret that omission and will constantly strive to seek legislation to that end via the Criminal Code or any other avenue. I was assured that the Charter at least did not worsen the present position and did not open the door to abortion on demand, etc. The reputable firm of lawyers consulted by the CCCB upheld that contention. While other respectable views are on record I could not honestly state that there was in my view a clear religious or moral opposition between the Church and the Charter.

Ours is the right and the duty to point out the issues in terms of gospel principles and Christian practice, not to enter the political arena. This position is strictly in conformity with the directives given by Pope John Paul II at Puebla and in Brazil."

That same day, Campaign Life sent out a news release reiterating its request that the Catholic Church oppose the Charter. It stated in part:

"Cardinal Carter on behalf of the Catholic Bishops and the Catholic church must speak out publicly in opposition to the Charter before the final vote in Parliament. Anything short of this is totally unacceptable to Campaign Life.

Cardinal Carter speaking on behalf of the Catholic Church and the Catholic Bishops of Canada has done irrevocable harm to Pro-Life efforts to persuade MPs to oppose the Charter because of its exclusion of protection for the unborn. By publicly removing his opposition to the Charter shortly

before the expected closure vote in Parliament on April 2,
and at the same time attempting to discredit Campaign Life,
Cardinal Carter cleared the way for Liberal MPs to ignore
Pro-Life protests."[16]

Journalist Claire Hoy put his finger on the problem with Cardinal Carter's clarification when he wrote in the *Toronto Sun* on April 30, 1981:

"Carter, in his ad, is trying to have it both ways, agreeing to
make Trudeau's task easier, while at the same time assuring
his flock he's still in there fighting for them."

Despite Cardinal Carter's "clarification", the CCCB apparently continued to have concerns about its support of the Charter. Bishop Adam Exner of Kamloops, Bishop Lawrence P. Wilhelm of Kingston, and Bishop Thomas Fulton of St. Catharines, issued statements expressing their unease about the future interpretation of the Charter.

Indeed, even before Carter's statement of April 4, 1981 in support of the Charter, Archbishop MacNeil of Edmonton, President of the CCCB had written to Trudeau, on March 26, 1981, stating:

"There remains one question which we consider to be of pri-
mordial importance; this relates to the respect for human
life which this Charter will embody. Thus, we respectfully
request, Mr. Prime Minister, that before your government fi-
nalizes the process of patriation with the entrenched Charter
of Rights and Freedoms, assurance be given to the Canadian
public that this Charter is intended to enhance the respect
for life from its very beginnings.

It would be deplorable if your Charter of Rights could either
now or in the future be interpreted in such a way as to broad-
en the impact and effect of the present abortion legislation
which is already in some of its prescriptions unacceptable to
us. Any Charter of Rights which is not founded upon respect
for life from the moment of conception would be flawed by
an inherent weakness.

I believe that not only the Roman Catholic community but
millions of other Canadians would appreciate a clear state-
ment from the Government on this matter." [17]

In a background paper, drafted by MP Douglas Roche (PC, Edmonton-Strathcona/ Edmonton South) subsequent to Archbishop MacNeil's letter, it was proposed that the concerns of the CCCB could be allayed by way of a clear statement written into the Charter. The paper proposed:

> *"One of the most effective ways of preventing the present proposed charter from being used to support abortion on demand is to have legislators make clear statements clarifying the intent of the Charter."*

Trudeau ignored Archbishop MacNeil's concerns until sometime after Carter's supporting announcement. Then, on April 24, 1981, he responded to Archbishop MacNeil stating that the government would not favour one side or the other of the [abortion] question.[18]

On May 26, 1981, Archbishop MacNeil wrote yet again to Trudeau stating that much opinion states that further interpretations will remove all protections to the right to life of unborn children:

> *"There is reasonable uncertainty. You acted on comparable uncertainty with native groups and separate school supporters.*
>
> *I believe that similar action should be taken in this matter."*

I ask:

> *"that your government introduce an amendment to the Charter, which would guarantee that the Charter would not prejudicially affect the rights of the unborn. Such action on the part of your Government would seem to be in accord with your intention to entrench the protection of life as expressed in section 7 of the Charter."* [19]

The Archbishop's letter was published in the *Toronto Star* June 5, 1981 and the *Catholic Register* on June 6, 1981. On June 6, 1981, Progressive Conservative MP Douglas Roche asked the government if it intended to comply with the request of the CCCB for an amendment to the Charter. Trudeau replied to Archbishop MacNeil rejecting his request stating:

> *"Because the public is evenly divided on the subject of abortion it was the government's "considered view" that "a position favouring one side should not be enshrined in the charter. The Government feels the issue of abortion is not one which should be defended by the Constitution."*[20]

On July 6, 1981, Trudeau wrote another letter to Archbishop Mac-Neil in which he refused to change the Charter citing two reasons:

"First, on April 9 agreement was reached on the constitutional debate and one stipulation was that there will be no amendments during the debate which will take place once the Supreme Court of Canada has rendered its decision.

Secondly, the arguments advanced to show that the Charter will create an entitlement to abortion on demand have been clearly refuted in the opinion given by the Department of Justice. In my view, the need for an amendment has not been clearly demonstrated." (21)

Trudeau's position became the standard response for the Liberals from then on. For example, on August 5, 1981 Pierre Fortin, assistant to Jean Chrétien, replied to Kathleen Toth, president of Campaign Life stating the Charter would not be amended, using the two reasons Trudeau gave to the Archbishop MacNeil. (22)

The practical reality was that Trudeau had Cardinal Carter onside with the Charter, and he no longer needed to concern himself about the Catholic Church on the matter.

Nonetheless, some of the clergy still pushed MPs to strongly oppose the Charter. Writing in *Fatima Priest*, Messrs. Francis Alban and Christopher Ferrara noted:

"1981. Parliament was preparing to vote on the Constitution. With little time and a meagre few hands to help, Father Gruner set about to make the Catholic Members of Parliament an offer they would not soon forget. In a twenty-five page letter informing Catholic Members of Parliament of the real meaning behind the constitutional terms, Father Gruner quoted Pius XI's Casti Connubi condemnation of abortion and made the point that it was a parliamentarian's moral obligation to defend the unborn. Failure to do so would make them guilty of the abortion death of Canadian babies through the sin of omission. With the help of an unnamed Member of Parliament, Father Gruner managed to place on the desk of every Catholic MP the reminder that if they voted for the proposed constitution, that was without protection for the unborn, they were going to be guilty of

*mortal sin and would end up in Hell, unless they truly re-
pented later on.*

*To succeed in positioning an outside paper on the desk of
each MP was almost unheard of and the reaction from the
Speaker of the House was swift. In his bruised and battered
mini-office in downtown Ottawa, Father Gruner received a
phone call from no less a personage than Jeanne Sauve, then
Madame Speaker of the House, who demanded to know
how he gained access.*

*Jeanne Sauvé was a Catholic. Prime Minister Pierre Trudeau
was supposed to be Catholic but no longer practiced his religion. Cabinet Minister John Turner, later to be Prime Minister, was Catholic. Jean Chrétien, another future Prime Minister, was also supposed to be Catholic. All of them, together,
were about to carve in stone a constitution that did not protect the unborn, in direct opposition to the requirements of
their faith. All of them proceeded to make it de facto legal
to suffocate, burn and scissor a baby in half in its mother's
womb. The image of a cassock-wearing priest gaining access
to the inner sanctum of Parliament to challenge the consciences of Catholic MPs was intolerable to them.*

*After all, had not Cardinal Emmett Carter, a spokesman for
the Canadian Conference of Catholic Bishops, himself pulled
back from challenging them by telling his brother bishops
in Canada that they had no business interfering with government. Yet Father Nicholas Gruner had published, to the
embarrassment of His Eminence, the fact that twenty-four
western Bishops had condemned the lack of protection for
the unborn."* [23]

Fr. de Valk, through the *Life Ethics Centre* at St. Joseph's College,
University of Alberta, sent a telegram, signed by 1500 prominent
people, including western Catholic Bishops from BC to the
Manitoba-Ontario border, to Chrétien expressing their concern
that the Charter of Rights did not protect the rights of the unborn.
Full page advertisements were also placed in the *Ottawa Citizen*,
Le Droit (Ottawa), *Le Devoir* (Montreal), *Catholic Register*, *Western
Catholic Reporter*, *BC Catholic*, and *The Prairie Messenger*. [24]

On May 2, 1981 Campaign Life released a special bulletin asking
people to encourage bishops to publicly oppose the Charter.

"We must encourage the Catholic Bishops to speak out against it in such a way that those MPs who are supporting it will know that not only the Pro-Life movement is opposed to the Charter, but also that a major church is opposed to it for pro-life reasons.

The Bishops of Canada now appear to be relying on assurances from Mr. Trudeau and from their own legal firm saying that the Charter does not lock in abortion-on-demand. However, they are not certain and because they have been given reasonable doubt they clearly have sufficient reason to oppose the Charter.

Cardinal Carter has nullified the efforts of the pro-life movement in Canada to encourage MP's to conscientiously oppose the Charter. Liberal MPs have been using the Cardinal's statements as an excuse to ignore pro-life protests. Copies of the Cardinal's statements have been widely distributed to constituents by Liberal MPs as a justification for their stance on the Charter.

Furthermore, Cardinal Carter, in his clarifying statement of April 29, 1981, has backed up his earlier remarks on the Charter with reference to the authority of the Canadian Conference of Catholic Bishops. Because of this, the Canadian Bishops can no longer claim neutrality on the Charter. They have been brought into the political fray in such a way that they now appear to be supporting Cardinal Carter's statement that there is no moral opposition between the Church and the Charter." [25]

Campaign Life approached many Catholic groups to have them oppose the charter. These included the clergy, the Catholic Women's League, the Knights of Columbus, parliamentarians and others.

However, many resisted Campaign Life's entreaties because they believed the Church was supporting the Charter. Landolt said she went to meetings of the Catholic Women's League and the Knights of Columbus to explain the Charter. At one meeting of the Knights, the council concerned brought a lawyer who contradicted all Landolt's arguments. Many regarded the members of Campaign Life as alarmists. [26]

Toronto lawyer John Stephens wrote Ursula Appolloni on May 13, 1981 stating:

"I continue to be of the opinion that Mr. Chrétien is wrong and that this was an opportunity for you both to have changed the law to afford protection for the unborn. You have not and you will have to live with that, as I have to live with the fact I could not convince you otherwise.

I appreciate your sending me Mr. Chrétien's letter but I really do not think much of it nor do I think any Court will fathom that reasoning. It is too much like a drowning man clutching at straws." [27]

On May 20, 1981, Jim Hughes, Chairman of Campaign Life, Paul Dodds, Chairman, Campaign Life Ontario and Kathleen Toth, President, Campaign Life Canada wrote, yet again, to the Canadian Bishops:

"We appeal to the Bishops of Canada to clarify the position of the Catholic church on the proposed Charter through a public statement by the Canadian Conference of Catholic Bishops opposing the proposed Charter. We ask that this be done before it is too late, that is, before the Charter comes to a final vote in Parliament."

They explained the many reasons the bishops should oppose, including the harm being done to the unborn and the wording which would recognize only persons already born. [28]

Paul Formby, national coordinator for Campaign Life, wrote, on May 25, 1981, to supporters requesting them "to encourage Catholic Bishops and other religious leaders to speak out in opposition to the Charter". [29]

Dr. John Shea, past president of the Toronto Catholic Doctors' Guild wrote Archbishop MacNeil, Sept 20, 1981, stating that:

"The charter...clearly states that rights and freedoms, which arise from the nature of man and are his birthright from God simply because he is man, can be abrogated by the state. This clause of the Charter has established the legal basis of the formation of a totalitarian state.

In view of the evils for society which may emanate from the adoption of a constitution which could lead to tyranny, and which certainly could be used by the Government and Supreme Court of Canada to allow or even promote such manifest wrongs as abortion and euthanasia, I feel it is the duty of the Catholic Bishops of Canada to speak out, loud and clear, on the essentially un-theistic and non-Christian nature of the Charter of Rights. The preamble recognizing the supremacy of God bears no relationship to the rest of the Charter.

It must also be publicly stated in unequivocal terms that the deliberate refusal of the Government of Canada to mention the unborn person's right to life in the constitution is a grievous moral evil...

This is a matter of profound moral and historical importance and I call upon the Canadian Bishops, before God, to act responsibly and to speak out before it is too late." [30]

On behalf of the CCCB, Dennis J. Murphy replied to Dr. Shea, Sept 24, 1981 telling him what Trudeau had previously told Archbishop MacNeil.

He then expressed interest in the "limits prescribed by law".

"It is certainly not a clause which heretofore has been brought to the attention of the CCCB as curtailing God given rights". [31]

Why did Cardinal Carter support the Charter?

Many were mystified why Cardinal Carter supported the Charter. They had their suspicions, however, as to what was behind this support.

These suspicions were first described in the *Catholic New Times* in April 1981 when columnist Janet Somerville wrote:

"Many think there must have been a three-way deal involving Cardinal Carter, Prime Minister Trudeau and Premier Davis, in which Cardinal Carter granted support for the Charter and got in exchange extension to Grade 13 of the separate school system in Ontario. The Chancery Office denies categorically that there was any deal at all behind the Cardinal's move on the Charter."

Columnist Tom Harpur, writing in the *Toronto Star* on April 11, 1981 stated:

"Dozens of interviews with anti-abortion spokesmen made it clear they believe the cardinal has made "some kind of a deal" with premier William Davis to extend more aid to separate schools (until then financed by Ontario up to Grade 10 only) and, as a result, was embarrassed politically by Campaign Life attacks on the Davis Tories during the recent election."

Kathleen Toth was quoted by *The Alberta Report*, on April 17, 1981, that a school deal had been made:

"Mrs. Toth suspects the Register's story represents 'a bit of a red herring', however. She is not alone in these suspicions. Last week rumours were rampant as stunned Catholics and pro-life workers across the country speculated on Cardinal Carter's real reason for dropping his opposition to the rights charter. Prominently favoured was the theory that he had made a deal with the Davis administration: the Ontario government would extend its financial support of separate schools to Grade 13 from Grade 10, and the cardinal would call off his troops on the Charter of Rights issue."

Catholic writer Anne Roche, writing in the same issue of the *Alberta Report*, April 17, 1981, thought Trudeau tricked Cardinal Carter:

"He's accepted some shop-worn assurances, it seems, which he's been suckered with before. The same promises were made in 1967 and 1968 when the Omnibus Bill came up, that abortion wouldn't be broadened, and they've been spectacularly broken. That was Mr. Trudeau's bill when he was Minister of Justice, it was passed after he became Prime Minister, and he assured Catholics that it would not broaden abortion. And now we're hearing him say the same thing about the rights charter. But of course it's going to, and we all know that it's going to."

Many continued to criticize Cardinal Carter in letters to the editor. One to the *Toronto Star* from Hank den Broeder suggested that Carter "return to the Bible". Another, in that same paper, from Hazel and John Douglas, members of the Peoples Church and Campaign Life supporters could not understand why Carter would say there are dangers to the unborn, but he would support it "because it has other unspecified advantages". [32]

There were other reasons to be suspicious about a deal with Premier Davis over enhanced funding for Catholic schools. During the 1981 Ontario provincial election, Campaign Life had placed an advertisement in the *Catholic Register*, published on April 26, 1981. The advertisement urged Catholics not to vote for Mr. Davis, the Progressive Conservative leader of Ontario because of the influential role he took in supporting the Charter. The advertisement stated that the Charter would result not only in abortion on demand, but also in same-sex marriages, homosexual adoptions, etc.

When the ad was published, Campaign Life received an angry phone call from Fr. A. J. (Angus) MacDougall, General Secretary of the Ontario Conference of Catholic Bishops demanding to know why Campaign Life was requesting that Catholics not vote for Premier Bill Davis. When it was explained that this was due to the fact that Mr. Davis was the "kingmaker" of the Charter's acceptance, Fr. MacDougall made no reply, and abruptly hung up the phone. If the Catholic Bishops had no stake in the re-election of Premier Davis, then why did they react so angrily to Campaign Life's advertisement during that provincial election?

Jim Hughes noted that Archbishop Carter was so furious at the *Catholic Register* that he fired the editor of the paper, Larry Henderson, because Henderson had listened to Campaign Life's side and said the bishops had lied to him. [33]

Cardinal Carter responded to the agitation against him and the CCCB by requiring all Catholic parishes in the Toronto archdiocese to ban information from Campaign Life. He also ordered the *Catholic Register* to no longer accept advertising from Campaign Life. Cardinal Carter gave as his reasons for doing that:

> *"It has and continues to be the policy of the diocese not to intrude on the freedom of any group to express their opinion. It has, however, been the policy of the Diocese not to allow political literature to be distributed within the Churches. This policy has been applied to the literature of Campaign Life." (34)*

Fr. de Valk, principal of St. Joseph's College at the University of Alberta, denounced this action in a letter to *The Globe and Mail*, April 30, 1981:

"The attack upon Campaign Life by means of ecclesiastical prohibition which accompanies this opinion seems to indicate that the cardinal would like his archdiocese to believe that his opinion on the charter is the only legitimate one and that members of the Liberal party should not be held responsible for their actions – or lack of action – in regard to the unborn."

It should be pointed out that Cardinal Carter's explanation for the extension of the Catholic school funding by Mr. Davis was referred to in an article in *The Globe and Mail*, on September 28, 2007, written by Gordon Sanderson, a retired journalist from the *London Free Press*. He had been given access to Cardinal Carter's memoirs before the latter's death. According to Cardinal Carter's memoirs, the change in the policy on separate school funding occurred because his brother and also a Bishop, Alexander Carter of Sault Ste. Marie, Archbishop Philip Pocock of Toronto and Archbishop Plourde of Ottawa had talked often with Premier Davis about extending funding for Catholic schools. When Carter became Archbishop of Toronto this persuasion continued. Carter would praise Davis, invite him to the Cardinal's Dinner and the like. Davis told Carter in 1984 that he had come to a decision to extend funding for Catholic schools. Some of his family attended Catholic schools and he felt it was only fair. When he presented his plan to caucus, there was little disagreement. So he brought it to the legislature.[35]

The factual evidence about the extension of funding to Catholic schools

In 1971, Premier Davis had rejected a proposal to grant full funding to Ontario's Catholic high schools. However, a few months before he retired as Premier in 1984, one of his last major acts as premier, was to reverse his 1971 decision against the full funding of Catholic schools announcing that such funding would be provided to the end of grade thirteen.

What was so peculiar about the decision of Davis to extend Catholic school funding was how he did it. According to the biography of Davis, written by journalist Steve Paikin, the issue was not discussed either with his caucus or his cabinet. (36) Davis simply advised at a special meeting of his cabinet on June 12, 1984 that he had decided to extend Catholic school funding to grade XIII and later that day advised his caucus of his decision. The decision was his alone. His Minister of Education, Dr. Bette Stevenson, who strongly objected to this extension of funding, was not at that cabinet meeting. She learned of the decision by Premier Davis after he had publicly made the announcement.

The explanation by Davis for this decision was that "it was the right thing to do". Why? What had changed since 1971 when his government opposed the extension of Catholic school funding? This policy in 1971 was met with wide approval and the Tories increased their number of seats in the provincial election held that year.

The reason for this decision was never made clear. Four months after his announcement on Catholic school funding, on October 8, 1984, Davis surprised everyone by his announcement that he was retiring from political life.

The battle continues

In a letter to Canada's bishops Nov 12, 1981, Paul Formby of Campaign Life wrote a letter which linked the actions of the Catholic hierarchy to the changes made in Vatican II and the resulting failure of Catholic bishops in Canada to take a strong stand on moral issues:

> "It seems that over the past year our efforts have encountered increasing opposition. We expect opposition from our opponents...However, when we encounter such opposition from people whom we assume to be on our side, as we have over this past year, then we can only wonder why? Perhaps it is political or, perhaps it is philosophical?
>
> If it is political, then we do have some consolation in knowing that at least some of the bishops in Canada endorse our efforts, because they realize that unless Christian people are committed to vote on this basic issue there will be no changes either in the policies of the federal Liberal government or, in those of any other government.
>
> Or if the opposition is due to philosophy, then the evidence points to pluralism. Over the past six months in our efforts to persuade Catholic bishops to take a strong stand, a number of our people have been confronted with the argument of

pluralism; i.e. "We cannot impose our morality on others." Since the 1960s when pluralism came into fashion, Roman Catholic legislators have generally echoed this argument whenever there has been a conflict between Christians and secular morality. Instead of Christian values being maintained in society, we have witnessed an increasing trend of Catholic political figures being used as instruments in the hands of our opponents to impose secular-humanist values upon our society – all with less and less opposition from religious leaders. The Charter is simply another feature of the trend."[37]

Gwen Landolt, left, Pierre Trudeau, centre, and Marc Lalonde in a May 1979 meeting.

Ontario Premier Bill Davis, (right) was all for a Charter of Rights while Joe Clark's Conservatives, were for the most part, not in favour.

According, to MP Garnet Bloomfield (above), during the charter debate, Trudeau advised his caucus that he was concerned about the growing impact of the pro-life movement to resist an entrenched Charter of Rights.

Chief Justice of the Supreme Court of Canada, Bora Laskin, who should have stayed neutral on the Charter debate, instead played a great part on both sides of the Atlantic in the repatriation the Constitution.

Pierre Trudeau, Allan MacEachen and Rene Levesque at the November 1981 constitutional conference in Ottawa.

Queen Elizabeth signs the Canadian Charter of Rights and Freedoms as Prime Minister Pierre Trudeau looks on smiling on April 17, 1982.

Pierre Trudeau and the provincial premiers after the signing of the Charter.

One of the few dissenting Provincial Premiers against the Charter was Manitoba's Sterling Lyon.

Cardinal Gerald Emmett Carter had issued a statement to the *Catholic Register* to the effect that he is convinced the Charter is neutral on the subject of abortion. He proved to be wrong.

Toronto lawyer John Stephens, above, and Gwen Landolt, legal counsel for Campaign Life, met with the pro-life caucus in February 1981 and warned them of the impact of the charter on the abortion issue.

Toronto lawyer Angela Costigan argued for the defence in a number of high profile abortion related court cases in the late 80's and early 90's. (See p. 180)

The Supreme court said there had to be a "substantial number" of provinces agreeing with the federal government's constitutional proposal. There were three dissenting judges in this decision who had concluded that Trudeau's unilateral resolution on the constitution was legal, despite its lack of provincial consent. The three judges were Mr. Justice Willard Estey (left) Mr. Justice William McIntyre, (right) and Chief Justice Bora Laskin.

Winifride Prestwich, a member of Campaign Life and a teacher at a private Toronto girls' school, accurately predicted that the fight against abortion was going to grow to be a fight against euthanasia and other moral issues.

Reverend Ken Campbell, founder of Renaissance International.

Kathleen Toth, first President of Campaign Life, founded in 1978, with her husband Mark.

Laura McArthur, second President of Toronto RTL, 1975-1991. Mrs. McArthur passed away in 1992.

Chapter 7

The Progressive Conservative party – divided on the Charter

Although the leader of the Progressive Conservative party, Joe Clark, supported the Charter, many members of his caucus did not.

The issue was so divisive within the caucus that it was agreed that the party would recommend the government first seek repatriation of the Constitution from the U.K., and then, once it had been returned to Canada, debate the merits of a Charter of Rights.

According to the polls, this approach was supported by the public. The *Toronto Star*, on January 14, 1981, released a poll which showed that 64% of Canadian adults would prefer to see the constitution turned over intact to Canada so that any changes or a charter could be approved here. Only 22% supported the inclusion of a Bill of Rights before the British North America Act was returned to Canada. 67% in Ontario and 61% in Quebec regarded this as the appropriate approach to the constitutional question.

A Gallup poll, published in the *Toronto Star* on February 14, 1981, showed that Trudeau and his constitution and charter of rights were becoming less popular. The poll noted:

Trudeau	September 1980	November 1980	January 1981
Approve	50%	45%	43%
Disapprove	35%	40%	46%

This was the reason why the Liberals, in contrast to the opposition PCs, wished to ram through the Charter as soon as possible. They did not want to have a debate on the merits of the Charter because this would raise the strong possibility that the Charter would never be passed.

One good reason for this fear was that there were many MPs who claimed to be pro-life and who rejected the Charter for this reason. On April 7, 1981, the Family Survival Fund wrote to MPs saying there were 152 pro-life MPs:

> "*Fifty-five Liberal MPS, fifty Conservatives and seven NDP MPs signed a written commitment that they would work to repeal the Criminal Code so as to give recognition to the right to life of the unborn and to institute or support legislation which would protect the lives of Canada's unborn children. It is also estimated that at least forty other elected MPs gave verbal assurances that they would also work to this end.*" [1]

No constitution or charter of rights had a chance of passing unless these 152 MPs changed their minds.

The Progressive Conservative party had good reason to be concerned about the implications of the proposed Charter. Its research office on March 12, 1981, identified 13 major opponents to Trudeau's constitutional resolution. They were:

> *Gallup poll says only 22% approve of government's unilateral action in trying to bring an amended constitution to Canada from Britain.*
>
> *8 of 10 provinces oppose the action; only Ontario and NB support it*
>
> *6 provinces are fighting the action in the courts*
>
> *Quebec Liberal leader Claude Ryan is totally opposed*
>
> *NDP in Saskatchewan, Alberta, Manitoba and Quebec have publicly spoken against the action*
>
> *4 NDP MPs will vote against it*
>
> *Ottawa West NDP association called on Broadbent to oppose the Trudeau package*
>
> *3 Liberal senators have spoken against package (Deschatelets, Thompson, Cook)*
>
> *2 Liberal MPs have opposed parts of the package (Duclos, Gauthier)*

Maxwell Cohen, a Liberal expert witness, spoke against it
Gordon Robertson, Trudeau's top constitutional advisor has
spoken against it
British inter-party committee has condemned the Trudeau
package
International committee of the British Labour party has
condemned it [2]

Further, many within the Progressive Conservative caucus were deeply concerned about the impact of the Charter on the abortion law and began to agitate publicly against it.

For example, on February 20, 1981 PC MP Douglas Roche stated he would oppose the Charter if it provided the right to abortion.[3]

On April 21, 1981 Gordon Taylor (PC Bow River), demanded that S.15 of the Charter include the unborn child.

On March 5, 1981 Thomas Siddon (PC Burnaby-Richmond-Delta) said:

> *"This charter of rights would perpetuate second-class citizenship upon many Canadians...There is the question of the rights of the unborn child contained within his or her mother's womb. Who has the right to life: the mother or the child? Who has the final say?"* [4]

Campaign Life worked with these MPs to consolidate opposition to the charter.

Once Trudeau obtained the agreement of the provinces (except for the province of Quebec) for a Charter on November 5, 1981, the already heated debate over the abortion issue within the Progressive Conservative caucus intensified. The disagreement was resolved by the caucus agreement that MP David Crombie who was supposedly "neutral" on the abortion issue (pro-life people knew otherwise) would propose an amendment to the Charter to ensure that it would not impact on the abortion issue.

On November 27, 1981 David Crombie proposed the following motion:

> *"That the proposed Constitution Act 1981 be amended by adding after clause 31 of Part 1 the following new clause:*
> *32. Nothing in this charter affects the authority of Parliament to legislate in respect to abortion."*

On speaking to his amendment, Mr. Crombie stated:

> "*The other day the Hon. Member for Etobicoke-Lakeshore (Mr. Robinson) asked the Prime Minister (Mr. Trudeau) a question with respect to this matter. The Prime Minister responded in this fashion:*
>
> *'If the essence of the question is whether this House continues to have the right to deal with abortion, Madam Speaker, the answer is yes. It will be the Parliament of Canada which will still be writing the Criminal Code, and members of this house will have the responsibility, and I wish them well, in dealing with the problem of abortion.'*
>
> *In my view, all sides of the House and, indeed, Canadians across the country want to ensure that Parliament has the right to legislate if any changes are deemed necessary with respect to the law on abortion. The difficulty for a great number of Canadians is that conflicting legal difficulties throw that matter into doubt. We want to make it clear that Parliament's freedom to legislate on this matter is unimpaired.*"[5]

Trudeau replied to Crombie's motion with his customary obfuscation about the abortion issue. He stated:

> "*Any further amendment such as the one presented by the Hon. Member...is actually a threat to the accord concluded on November 5...*
>
> *The Minister of Justice (Mr. Chrétien) has explained several times in this House, in point and verbally on other occasions, that in his view, which is supported by his own Department of Justice, the charter is at this point in time neutral with respect to abortion. In other words, the charter does not say whether abortions will be easier or more difficult to practice in the future. The charter is absolutely neutral on this matter, and according to the interpretation of senior officials and agents of the Department of justice and according to the minister himself, under the constitution the House retains the right to amend the Criminal Code, which is the statute affecting the issue of abortion...*
>
> *Should a judge conclude that...the charter does, to a certain extent, affect certain provisions of the Criminal Code, un-*

der the override clause we reserve the right to say: Notwithstanding this decision, notwithstanding the charter of rights as interpreted by this judge, the House legislates in such and such a manner on the abortion issue.

This amendment is not only unnecessary but could, indeed, be harmful because, by excluding from the charter the right to do something as regards abortion, lawyers and judges might be inclined to conclude that since we made that exclusion for abortion and did not make it for euthanasia, capital punishment and so on, therefore the charter itself precludes the Parliament of Canada from legislating in these areas."[6]

Trudeau then declared that Liberal MPs would not support Crombie's amendment.[7]

When the speaker called the vote, 60 voted for Crombie's motion and 129 voted against it. Several Liberal MPs, however, refused to follow Trudeau's orders and voted for Crombie's amendment. They were Peter Lang, Stan Hudecki, Paul McRae, Garnet Bloomfield, Bob Bockstael and George Baker. New Democrats voting in favour of Crombie's motion were Doug Anguish and Bob Ogle, a Catholic priest.[8]

What was generally not known at that time was that the agreement within the PC caucus to present Crombie's amendment as a compromise on the Charter was that should the amendment fail, then the entire caucus would vote for the Charter. This agreement created a moral dilemma for pro-life PC MPs. On the one hand they were bound by caucus agreement to vote for the Charter if Crombie's motion failed, but how could pro-life MPs reconcile such a vote with their consciences?

This moral dilemma was handled differently by individual PC MPs.

Jake Epp, a prominent pro-life MP, explained his decision to vote for the constitutional amendment in a letter dated November 26, 1981 to a constituent:

"I am satisfied that after careful consideration and consultation the recent Constitutional Accord has upheld the PC position (that no decision by Parliament with regard to the right to life for the unborn should be changed by an interpretation (in the courts) of the Charter of Rights. Regardless of

any court's interpretation of Section 15 or 7 of the Charter, Parliament has the final and supreme authority to legislate with respect to the right to life." [9]

In effect Mr. Epp believed that the Charter did not constitute a threat to the unborn, and if it did, protection could be provided by Parliament. He therefore was free to vote for it.

Pro-life MP Peter Elzinga (PC Pembina) stated in a letter dated December 10, 1981 to Kathleen Toth, President of Campaign Life that "he believed Trudeau that Parliament would still have complete power in dealing with the Constitution." [10]

David Kilgour (PC Edmonton) had previously taken a prominent position opposing the Charter because of the abortion issue. For example, in a demonstration on Parliament Hill on October 13, 1981 Mr. Kilgour had stated:

"Jean Chrétien (Minister of Justice) knows what it means and Pierre Trudeau knows what it means, and so do all others in the House with legal training. Pointing his finger at the House he said they all knew that the Charter locks in abortion-on-demand." [11]

However, in the end he voted for the Charter, explaining why he did so in a letter addressed to Kathleen Toth:

"In my legally trained mind, there developed an implied agreement that if David Crombie would move the amendment, which would presumably hurt him in swinging parts of Rosedale, those of us in caucus who felt so strongly about the subject would later vote for the resolution regardless of the outcome of the House vote on our amendment. Obviously, on the basis of his vote, Doug Roche and other pro-life Tories who voted "no" did not share my outlook on this agreement." [12]

MP Douglas Roche voted against the Charter solely for conscience reasons.

Mr. Roche told the authors of this book in a personal interview on November 1, 2012 that nothing that he had ever done in his long professional life as a newspaper editor, MP, Minister of Disarmament, and as a Senator, gave him more satisfaction than his vote against the Charter.

Former MPs Epp and Kilgour declined to be interviewed for this book.

Chapter 8

Opposition to the Charter during 1981

Throughout 1981, the struggle to protect the unborn in the Charter of Rights intensified.

On Jan 21, 1981, Gwen Landolt of Campaign Life wrote Jake Epp regarding the changes proposed by Chrétien. After noting Chrétien's proposal and the dangers it posed to the unborn, she asked Epp to propose two amendments:

> *S.7 Everyone from the moment of conception onwards, who is innocent of any crime, has the absolute right to life. Everyone has the right to liberty and security of person, and the right not to be deprived thereof, except in accordance with the principles of fundamental justice.*
>
> *S.15(1) Every individual from the moment of conception onwards is equal before and under the law and has the right to the equal protection and equal benefit of the law without discrimination and in particular without discrimination based on race, national or ethnic origin, colour, religion, sex or age.*

She also requested that he request a new section to precede Section 27:

Nothing in this Charter affects the authority of Parliament to legislate in respect of abortion and capital punishment.

Epp subsequently proposed amendments to the Charter including recognizing:

"the sovereignty of God over the nation, the family as the cornerstone of society and the right to own personal property" and that "nothing in the Charter will affect the authority of Parliament to legislate in respect to abortion and capital punishment." [1]

Bob Ogle, (NDP Saskatoon East), a Catholic priest:

"pleaded with the committee to accept Mr. Epp's suggestion saying Canada "was founded by people who, on the whole, believed in God."

Svend Robinson, NDP, rejected it saying:

"inclusion would be contrary to the right of freedom of conscience which includes the right to have no religion or be an atheist."

Liberal Bob Kaplan, Solicitor-General, said the preamble should contain even more values, so the Liberals would oppose it. He noted they were "not opposed to God but to a preamble in general".[2]

Fr. de Valk wrote a letter to the *Western Catholic Reporter* on Jan 26, 1981 entitled "Charter Clearly Denies Rights". Copies of this letter were mailed to all MPs, MLAs, weekly papers and church leaders.

In the letter, Fr. de Valk noted that among the 100 briefs presented during the televised hearings, at least four briefs – three from national pro-life groups and one from the Ontario bishops – requested that the charter provide protection for the unborn.

"Political expediency appears to be all that counts. The Liberal party stands ready …for its second – and quite possibly – final betrayal of the Canadian people."

He asked Catholics and all Christians to stop voting Liberal.

Fr. de Valk closed by noting how clear the Liberal intention was:

"The following note was found among the section-by-section explanations: section 15.1: 'Everyone' is replaced by 'every individual' to make it clear that this right would apply only

to natural persons. The root form of natural is the Latin natus, i.e. born. Thus the intention of the government is perfectly clear."

On Feb 9, 1981, Serge Joyal (L, Hochelaga/Maisonneuve) wrote to Landolt saying "be assured that I will consider your point of view concerning the section 15(1) of the Charter".[3] He considered and rejected it.

On Feb 12, 1981, pro-life MP Robert Bockstael, (Liberal St. Boniface) asked Mildred Morton, Research Branch, Law and Government Division, to explain the three terms "everyone", "individual" and "person". Morton stated that all three did not recognize the unborn. If rights were wanted, "legislation must provide for these rights now".[4]

Unfortunately, the pro-abortion side was moving fast against these pressures, especially the organized and government-supported feminist groups. In February 1981, the feminist Ad Hoc Women's Conference in Ottawa recommended the following amendment to the Charter:

This Charter shall apply equally to male and female persons.

On Thursday April 21, 1981, the NDP brought forward the amendment in support of the feminists' request. It was accepted by the Liberals and drafted by the Justice Department to become s.28:

Notwithstanding anything in this Charter, the rights and freedoms referred to in it are guaranteed equally to male and female persons.

In a newsletter of April 15, 1981, Campaign Life warned that the amendment proposed by the Liberals and NDP would remove protection for the unborn:

"With this amendment any doubt as to the intention of the government to lock in abortion-on-demand has been swept away. This is based on the fact that, as you know, the word 'person' has already been defined by the US Supreme Court so as to exclude the unborn child."

Trudeau's strategy in regard to the Charter and the abortion issue was clear. He requested and obtained a legal opinion from the Justice Department to state, in effect, that the Charter would not affect the abortion issue. Trudeau and his party then doggedly promoted this partisan legal opinion as a self-evident, incontrovertible truth. Trudeau encouraged prominent well-known pro-life MPs and Senators to promote this partisan legal opinion provided by the Justice Department. The simple message was that if these prominent individuals, who were pro-life, considered that the Charter did not endanger the life of the unborn child, then, of course, that must be so, and that those opposing them were unreasonable extremists.

On Feb 6, 1981, The Right to Life Association of Toronto and Area issued an Urgent Statement on the Proposed Constitution, entitled, *"Analysis of the Proposed Constitution and how it will affect the Rights of the Unborn Child in Canada"*. It stated that it offered no protection to the unborn, would result in a horrendous increase in abortions and would put laws under the control of an appointed group – the Supreme Court.

The Catholic school question

Gwen Landolt, as Legal Counsel for the Right to Life Association of Toronto and Area, tried on several occasions to convince Legal Counsel for the Catholic School Board in Toronto, to make a submission to the Joint Committee on the Constitution to ensure that the Catholic Schools in Canada be specifically protected under the Charter of Rights. The Legal Counsel, however, insisted that this was not necessary, believing there was already sufficient protection for Catholic Schools provided under the British North America Act (BNA) of 1867. This was a dubious assumption.

Consequently, a brief was prepared explaining the threat to the Catholic Schools in Canada if there was no specific protection given them under the Charter. The Right to Life Association of Toronto and Area forwarded this brief to all the Catholic School Boards in Canada. This raised the alarm for Catholic School trustees and resulted in the Canadian Catholic School Trustee's Association appearing as a witness before the Committee requesting that protection be provided for the Catholic Schools in Canada in the Charter of Rights.

The Joint Committee accepted this recommendation by the Catholic Schools Trustees to amend the Constitutional Resolution to include specific protection for Catholic Schools. This amendment to the Charter reads as follows:

Section 29. There can be no abrogation or derogation from any rights or privileges guaranteed under the Constitution of Canada in respect of "denominational, separate or dissentient schools".

This provision provided legal protection for the continued existence of Catholic Schools when a number of legal challenges were subsequently brought against them under the Charter, arguing that Catholic schools were discriminatory and created inequality. Because of Section 29 of the Charter of Rights, these legal challenges were rejected by the courts.

Continuing demands for protection of the unborn

On Feb 12, 1981, Ottawa lawyer David Dehler wrote to James McGrath, (PC, St. John's East) copying Trudeau, Clark, Chrétien and many others, asking that "the abuse of language and vagueness about sec.15 and sec.7 be cleared up". He proposed specific changes. He asked that the right to life of every human being be explicitly spelled out. He pointed out that such clarity was in accordance:

"...with the United Nations Declaration of the Rights of the Child unanimously approved by the United Nations in Plenary Session in 1959, and renewed in May 1968 at the International Human Rights Conference". [5]

On February 16, 1981, Kathleen Toth wrote a letter to *The Globe and Mail* in which she warned of the dangers in the proposed constitution:

"Are we to look forward to abortion on demand in Canada? Are we to expect the Supreme Court to order the establishment of abortion facilities in every community? Would hospitals receiving public funds be obliged to provide abortion facilities? Unless the phrase, 'right to Life' is put beyond the interpretation of the Supreme Court by inserting, "from the moment of conception onward', this charter of rights removes the power of Parliament to legislate on this issue. Nine appointees to the Supreme Court have the awesome power to strike down all existing legislation which seeks to provide some little protection to unborn babies.

The concessions made to the New Democratic Party include

those amendments which were attributed to the brief presented by the Advisory Council on the Status of Women. New Democrats know that their every hope has been realized if the charter of rights remains unchanged."

The Hamilton Right to Life asked members to write MPs. They worried about the courts:

"...we must point out the enormous power which the Supreme Court will acquire under the entrenchment of the Charter of Rights in the new Constitution. The nine members of the Court are appointed at the sole discretion of the Prime Minister and remain on the bench until 75 years of age. They are accountable to no one. It is not unreasonable to assume that the opinions expressed on important social issues such as abortion, will reflect only the personal views of these judges and not those of the general public. In short, the life or death of generations yet unborn, may depend on the personal view of five individuals (a bare majority of the Court). No appointed group should have such power. This power should belong only to Parliament, which is elected by, and responsible to, the people of Canada." [6]

Earl Amyotte, member of CLC and of Windsor Right to Life, published a letter in the *Windsor Star* March 16, 1981, calling for Parliament to restore legal protection for the unborn child and specifically asked MPs Mark MacGuigan and Eugene Whelan, who claimed to be pro-life, to deliver.

Toronto lawyer John Stephens wrote letters on March 3, 1981 and again on March 26, 1981 to all the MPs repeating his legal analysis of the problem. He wrote:

"A recent Canadian court case which stands for the proposition that a child en ventre sa mere must be born before it can assert rights.

Our review indicated that the use of words such as "person", "citizen", "everyone", "individual" or "human being" were really not relevant since to assert rights a fetus must be born.

Viewed in this light then the Charter of Rights does nothing to add to the existing law in which neither the fetus nor the father of the fetus has a right to interfere with an abortion sought by the mother carrying the fetus.

In fact by enshrining certain rights now, Parliament will be forever precluded from impinging on those rights unless the charter itself is amended."

The case was Dehler v. Ottawa Civic Hospital et al. (1979) referred to previously in which Mr. Justice Robins stated "the law has selected birth as the point at which the fetus becomes a person with full and independent rights." This decision was approved by the Ontario Court of Appeal and the Supreme Court refused the application to appeal.

Stephens concluded that section 7 had to be amended to read as follows:

"Every person (including the unborn), has the right to life (which life begins at conception and which right is assertable from conception)..." [7]

Section 7 was the major section in the Charter that the Supreme Court used to strike down the abortion law.

In the collection of documents sent Feb 27, 1981, to members of the House of Commons Pro-Life Committee, John Stephens warns that the use of "individual" will raise a number of anomalies:

a. *Since all distinction between male and female must be eliminated, it will permit marriage licenses to be issued to two persons of the same sex wishing to "marry";*

b. *Abortion services may be extended by court order to provide equal accessibility*

On March 4, 1981 the *Toronto Star* noted that twenty MPs, half of them Liberals demanded written assurance from Jean Chrétien that the government's constitutional proposals would protect unborn children. Progressive Conservative MP Walter Dinsdale was co-chairman of the committee. Other members included Liberal David Weatherhead, and Bob Ogle, NDP.

Mr. Dinsdale (PC, Brandon) then asked Chrétien for legal opinions from the law officers of the Crown on sections 15 and 17, especially those "opinions that specifically address themselves to the abortion issue".[8]

The Justice Department responded:

"There are no provisions in the Charter of Rights which can affect present abortion laws in one way or another, or pre-

clude Parliament from enacting laws in the future dealing with the issue.

The existence of abortion clinics is dependent not on the Constitution but on the Criminal Code. If the Criminal Code is ever changed so as to prohibit abortion, no one could even make the argument that the 'equal protection clause' would apply so as to require the creation of abortion clinics."

This opinion deliberately ignored the central concern of the MPs. Of course, there was no provision in the Charter directly on abortion. It was the exclusive power given to the courts by the Charter that was the concern of the MPs. Under the Charter, the court could, as stated previously, also use its power to overturn the abortion law and could set down guidelines or restrictions on the application of any future abortion law. In short, instead of Parliament correcting or overturning the courts, the latter would have the power to overrule or correct Parliament. The Department of Justice lawyers obviously knew this, but chose to ignore it. Its opinion was designed to obscure, rather than to enlighten.

Trudeau not swayed

This obvious lack of confidence by the MPs and the general public in the proposed constitution did not sway Trudeau. He had little respect for elected MPs, and, therefore, had even less respect for the members of the public who had elected them. He ignored their concerns because he regarded them as uninformed and unable to grasp the supposed gift he was giving to the nation by way of his constitutional proposal. He naively believed his constitution was of enormous benefit because the courts could henceforth protect minority rights from the tyranny of the majority. Like many theorists, however, Trudeau was either unwilling or unable to consider the practical downside to his grand plan. The reality was that, as a result of the Charter, the courts were given an unhindered opportunity to dictate their own values and perspectives to the majority of the population. As a result of the Charter, the public became mere spectators or bystanders in the governing of Canada since it no longer had a role in influencing public policy by way of Parliament, the latter which had a diminished role in determining public policies. Trudeau also did not foresee that the courts would use their acquired power under the Charter to discover, in the vague wording of the Charter, completely new rights never before considered, or desired by the public.

A few days after the Justice Department had ruled, yet again, that the unborn child would be protected, the Right to Life Association of Toronto and Area released a newsletter stating that this interpretation was wrong:

> *"The Justice Department is wrong.*
>
> *The Appeal Court of Ontario, in the Dehler versus Ottawa Civic Hospital 1980, ruled that in Canada, the unborn child cannot exercise any legal rights, unless or until he/she is born alive.*
>
> *The Supreme Court of Canada, in February 1981 affirmed this decision.*
>
> *A precedent has been set; we no longer have to guess what a future court might rule. The Supreme Court of Canada, the highest court in the land, has decreed that the unborn child has no legal rights until birth.*
>
> *Since section 15 of the Charter of Rights, gives total and complete rights to women, and these rights are locked in the charter, any attempt to tighten the abortion laws would be regarded as an infringement upon these rights and, therefore, declared unconstitutional."* [9]

On March 24, 1981, Jean Chrétien, Minister of Justice and Attorney-General of Canada, wrote to Gwen Landolt explaining his position. He stated the change in s.7 from "everyone" to "every individual" was made to exclude corporate entities. He stated the Charter was neutral on abortion:

> *"I have emphasized on several occasions…that it is the policy of the government that the Charter of Rights remain neutral on the matter of abortion, neither entrenching a constitutional right to obtain an abortion nor entrenching a constitutional bar to the enactment of laws governing abortion. In other words,* **the Charter has been drafted in a manner which will leave to Parliament its present authority to deal with this important social and moral issue from time to time."** (Emphasis ours)

He did acknowledge that current law offered no protection for the unborn.

"In Canadian, American and British jurisprudence, the courts have consistently held that an unborn child (whether referred to as a "person" an "individual" or "everyone") does not acquire legal rights until after birth. It would seem evident that the Charter will be interpreted in light of this jurisprudence. Consequently, I do not see how the courts will infer any rights to the unborn under sections 7 or 15, whether it be a right to life or a right to equal protection or benefit of law."

Finally, he ended the letter saying he doubted the courts would establish a right to abortion:

"I am satisfied that the courts will not construe section 15 (or section 7) as establishing a constitutional right to abortion on demand or state-financed clinical facilities for such a purpose.

While the United States Supreme Court has construed the "due process" clause of that country's Bill of Rights as establishing a qualified right to obtain an abortion, the Charter of Rights does not include a similar clause which has permitted the American courts to adjudicate the substantive, as opposed to the procedural, quality and fairness of laws. Consequently, I am satisfied that the wording of the Charter will not permit our courts to find a constitutional right to obtain an abortion.

Equally, I am satisfied that the "equality clause" will not be construed as requiring the state to provide funds for the obtaining of abortions. You are not doubt aware that the United States Supreme Court has ruled in several cases that laws which provide state funding for medical care, including childbirth but not abortion treatment, are not in contravention of the "equality clause". In my view a similar result will pertain in Canada.

In consequence, it is my conclusion that the relevant provisions of the Charter as drafted will be interpreted in a manner consistent with the above-stated policy of the government: namely, that laws governing abortion will be determined by Parliament and not by judgments of the courts based on provisions of the Charter." [10]

Chrétien was completely wrong in these conclusions as determined by later events. The pro-life movement would not accept this argument presented by Chrétien. In a paper dated March 27, 1981 Gwen Landolt wrote a somber and accurate prediction:

> *"It is indeed an awesome fact that the principles of our Judeo-Christian heritage upon which Canada was built as a nation will no longer be guiding factors in our future. Historically, it was under our Judeo-Christian principles that Canada has flourished for 114 years and had guaranteed rights for everyone regardless of sex, race, and religion, as well as, an ennobling and enriching multicultural society. Under the Charter of Rights, Canada will officially become a secular state with the government being the unquestioned authority. As a result, our future may not be a secure one."* [11]

Campaign Life tries again

Campaign Life wrote to the Vatican hoping to move the Catholic bishops to oppose the Charter. It requested direct assistance for this from the Vatican after individuals within the Vatican had offered assurance that a letter to Pope John Paul II on this issue would be placed before him for his immediate attention. Campaign Life's letter to Pope John Paul II, dated May 12, 1981, stated:

> *"By publicly removing his opposition to the Charter, Cardinal Carter has completely undermined the work of the pro-life movement in Canada to insure protection for the unborn in the Charter. All our efforts to encourage Members of Parliament to oppose the Charter have been nullified. The government has used the Cardinal's statement in Parliament and in special letters to constituents, to deflect enquiries and protests regarding the exclusion of the right to life for the unborn in the Charter.*
>
> *It is also our view that the Catholic Hierarchy in Canada now has a responsibility to make clear what the position of the Catholic Church is on the Charter.*
>
> *The Archdiocese of Toronto needs an Archbishop who will truly stand up for the right to life of the unborn. Our country needs strong and courageous religious leaders who will speak out publicly on behalf of pro-life."* [12]

This same letter was also sent to all the Catholic bishops in Canada.

Three days later, on May 15, 1981, Pope John Paul II was shot in an assassination attempt in Saint Peter's Square. His life hung in the balance for many weeks and it took a year for him to recover from his wounds.

The Pope's reply came only in May of 1982, one month after the new Constitution Resolution was proclaimed on April 17, 1982. Campaign Life received a letter from Fr. John Day, Personal Secretary to Pope John Paul II. The letter stated that the Pope had read Campaign Life's material, thanked Campaign Life for its effort on behalf of the unborn child, and extended his blessings. It was too late. What was done was cast in stone.

Although the pro-life movement's efforts to have the Catholic Bishops oppose the Charter were unsuccessful, this did not deter it from working tirelessly in other directions to achieve its goal of protecting the unborn from the Charter.

Landolt wrote a paper on the *Charter of Rights and Traditional Values* on April 20, 1981. She warned that "An entrenched Bill of Rights in the Constitution cannot be changed by Parliament."

> *"The rights of Canadians will now be defined and interpreted by the courts only. No longer will there be 'inalienable rights endowed by the Creator to every human being created in the image of God'. Under the Charter of Rights, Canada officially becomes a secular state with the government being all powerful and the source of all 'justice' without resorting to a Higher Being.*
>
> *Pro-life lawyers across Canada advise that abortion on demand, although not expressly so stated, has been locked into the Charter of Rights by reason of the wording of certain sections of the Charter."*

She identified other results, including:

1. Loss of special recognition in employment.
2. Women would be required to be equal to men regardless of their physical differences: e.g., weight, strength, etc.
3. Loss of parental rights over minors
4. Homosexual marriage and adoption
5. Loss of property rights [13]

Campaign Life ran a large ad in the *Toronto Star* on April 26, 1981, denouncing the "Charter of Injustice". The ad stated precisely that the Charter would lead to abortion on demand, homosexual marriage and adoption, loss of rights for women (freedom from hazardous jobs, such as combat duty, no segregated washrooms and dorms, etc.), and loss of democratic freedom. It was eerily correct in these predictions. Campaign Life blamed Trudeau for imposing the Charter on the people, without their knowledge or consent.

Lobbying of both the Conservative and Liberal MPs continued with considerable success. The lobbying was organized by one of its members who had a large home located in the Glebe area of Ottawa – just a few blocks from Parliament Hill. She furnished accommodation and meals and organized the many lobbyists who came from across Canada. She assigned the lobbyists each day to the MPs and kept a record of the position taken by each MP on the constitutional resolution. It was a well-organized effective lobby.

MP Jake Epp (PC Provencher), the party's constitutional spokesman, stated in March 1981 that he was receiving up to 1000 letters a day from Canadians expressing concern over Trudeau's actions on the Constitution.

Six hundred people from Alberta signed a letter by Kathleen Toth to all MPs asking them to:

> *"point out the necessity of including the specific wording in Section 15(1): "Every individual" should be changed to "Every individual from the moment of conception onward" is equal before and under the law..."* [14]

An English/French organization of pro-life women headed by Jean Morse-Chevrier from Quebec and Grace Cameron from Ottawa formed the organization called the Ad Hoc Committee of Pro-Life Women. This organization consisted of organizations such as the Catholic Women's League, the *Front Commun pour le respect pour la vie, le Conseil de la Famille du Quebec* and Campaign Life. They represented about 500,000 members. They held a press conference for a large section of the media including CBC radio and TV, French and English, CTV and daily newspapers in many parts of the country. The Committee denounced the Charter saying it did not protect the unborn and would allow the courts to impose abortion on demand. They demanded that MPs be allowed to vote on the package as their consciences dictated.

The bias typical of the media on the abortion issue was apparent in that the CBC did not mention it while the CTV only mentioned it for a few seconds. The *Toronto Star* had a brief article on it. [15] Only one other media outlet covered the story.

Mr. Chrétien confirmed that the Charter provided an equivalent of the ERA amendment on CTV when he was interviewed by broadcaster Pamela Wallin on October 16, 1981. Mr. Chrétien stated:

> *"But you have rights Madam. In the United States the women are fighting since years to have the ERA amendment in the constitution. I'm giving it to the Canadian women right away, but some premiers want to peddle your rights against their own power, that they would like to have a bigger. (sic) Are you not offended?"* [16]

On October 26, 1981, Campaign Life informed Canadians of the dangers of sections 15 and 28:

> *"If these two sections become entrenched in the Canadian Constitution then Canada will be changed and altered so dramatically that we will, in fact, be living in a completely new social system. It is significant that these two 'equal rights' sections are even broader and more far-reaching than that of the extremely controversial U.S. Equal Rights Amendment (ERA) which, as you know, was* **rejected** *by the American people in the 1980 presidential election."*

It explained how these sections would affect abortion:

> *"1. Section 15 provides that every individual will have 'full benefit of the law'. S.15 will be used by the pro-abortionists to argue before the courts that women are being discriminated against in localities where hospitals do not provide abortions. Thus they are thereby being denied equal access to the alleged 'benefit' of the abortion law. It is important to note that under another amendment to the Charter proposed by Mr. Chrétien, January 12, 1981, the court will be empowered to apply 'remedies' as it considers 'just and appropriate'. Thus, if the court determines that there is discrimination under*

s.15, it could order a certain hospital to provide abortions, or, it could even go further by ordering the provincial Minister of Health to widen the access to abortion by requiring him to 'approve' more hospitals for abortion, i.e. establish abortion clinics, as the Minister of Health is empowered to do under s.251 (5) of the Criminal Code.

2. The inclusion of the word 'person' in s.28 of the Charter categorically denies any protection to the unborn child. This is based on the fact that in the U.S. the Supreme Court abortion decision Roe v. Wade, *the court held that 'person' did not include the unborn child.* Roe v. Wade *has been quoted with approval by Canadian courts in* Dehler v. Ottawa Civic Hospital *which held that the unborn child had no right until birth.*

These sections would affect the traditional Canadian family in various ways. Women would lose legal protection in marriage. They could lose rights such as maternity leave. They could lose rights in the workplace. Same sax marriage will be promoted. Same sex couples will be allowed to adopt children." [17]

Campaign Life demonstrated on Parliament Hill on October 13 & 16, 1981 then from October 19 to 30 They also picketed Liberal Cabinet Ministers in their home ridings. Among those who spoke at the October 13, 1981 demonstration were MPs Jake Epp, PC spokesman on the constitution, and David Kilgour, (PC, Edmonton), both of whom ultimately voted for the Charter. [18]

On November 12, 1981 Paul Formby of Campaign Life appealed to the Canadian Conference of Catholic Bishops once again to speak out:

"During the annual meeting of the Conference of Catholic Bishops in Ottawa, October 26-29, a number of pro-life representatives, including our National president from Edmonton, approached as many individual Bishops as possible, imploring them to take a stand on the Charter. Although a certain number of the bishops were receptive and supportive, the general reaction that the pro-life representatives received was that the bishops were not really concerned and that as a body nothing would be done." [19]

Although established pro-life groups such as Campaign Life were interdenominational, there were also faith-based groups who joined with it in the effort to provide protection for the unborn child in the Charter.

Renaissance International

Renaissance was founded in 1974 by Rev. Ken Campbell, a determined and charismatic pastor who was a member of the Evangelical Baptist Church in Ancaster, Ontario. His political involvement was initially triggered by his concern about the Halton Region education system relating to parental rights, and the reading materials provided for children in the schools as well as sex education in the schools where his five children were in attendance. He subsequently expanded his interest to the issues of homosexuality and the abortion issue and the Charter of Rights.

His concern was identical to that of Campaign Life – namely, that the Charter would enable the courts to strike down the already wide abortion law, leaving unborn children without legal protection.

Reverend Ken Campbell and his supporters from across Canada began to heavily lobby politicians from all parties. He placed full page ads opposing the Charter in the *Toronto Sun* and *The Globe and Mail* in early 1981.

In a newsletter issued in February 1981, Reverend Campbell denounced the Charter:

> *"And now as we begin this new year which finds our nation in the throes of the greatest crisis since confederation – with leadership bent on tearing this country from its foundations of freedom in our Judeo-Christian heritage, and the imposition on a free people of a secular, centralized, socialist state – the Lord has sent us to rebuke such wickedness in high places and to call a nation back to the ways of the Lord."*

He printed a report in all major newspapers from Ottawa to Vancouver. He published over one million copies of his advertisement.

Rev. Campbell, on behalf of "Canadians for Freedom with Honour" and as "Canada's moderate majority", then wrote to Edward Schreyer, the Governor General of Canada, stating that the Supreme Court decision, our written and unwritten laws and conventions are being ignored by Trudeau whose:

"...defiance of the constitutional restrictions on his arbitrary behaviour is posing an unprecedented threat to Canadian unity and/or the survival of Confederation."

He petitioned the Governor General:

"In accordance with your constitutional powers:

You take action at once to remove from Mr. Trudeau the unwritten constitutional rights and privileges accorded to the Prime Minister of Canada; (which unwritten conventions Mr. Trudeau himself refuses to recognize in our constitution);

And/or

You dissolve Parliament at once and issue writs for a general election." [20]

As a result of the efforts of Renaissance, the Liberals had the Department of National Revenue threaten its tax exempt status. In his February newsletter, Campbell notes that he received a threatening letter from the Taxation Department of National Revenue:

"You are hereby notified that I propose to revoke the registration of Renaissance International...As it has devoted resources to activities that are not charitable activities.

E.A. Chater, Director, Registration Division, Department of National Revenue, Taxation"

Reverend Campbell also blamed this development on complaints from the homosexual lobby:

"I want to know how a militant homosexual crusader, masquerading as an aldermanic candidate, (George Hislop, a leading spokesperson for militant homosexuals, solicited funds for his 'aldermanic campaign' in Toronto's Ward 6 in the Fall of 1980, among flaunting homosexuals coast to coast), by his unfounded, widely publicized charges against a pro-family religious charity (which had dared to publicly defend the integrity of the family from the destructive intents of 'the horribly menacing gay lobby' represented by Mr. Hislop and several other candidates in the 1980 Metro Municipal Elections), can apparently instigate immediate deregis-

tration action by a government agency against that charity? Look at the central page of today's Sun *(Feb 1, 1981) – the controversial Renaissance International is having its registration as a charitable organization revoked because it actively opposes homosexuals becoming incorporated deeper into schools and daily life"* [21]

Reverend Ken Campbell, along with Reverend Ron Marr of the *Christian Enquirer,* organized a Canada in Crisis Rally on March 7, 1981 at Massey Hall in Toronto. Among attendees at the Crisis in Canada rally were Bev LaHaye of Family Life Seminar in the US, Conservative MPs David Kilgour and John Gamble, Gwen Landolt, legal counsel and Jim Hughes of Campaign Life, Rev William Hiltz of the Freedom of Religion Committee, Diane Lee of Edu-Action Ontario, Harry Barrett of Citizens for Responsible Education, Stu Newton of Positive Parents, and others.

In an ad in the *Toronto Sun,* March 15, 1981, Reverend Campbell warned the public to be careful who they voted for. He denounced Ontario premier Davis for supporting abortion, undermining Christian education in Ontario, caving in to the demands of the militant fringe of the homosexual movement, undermining the freedom of religion, refusing to preserve the Judeo-Christian heritage, and the transfer of control to the courts.

He objected to Davis' support of Mr. Trudeau's "charter of injustice" which he claimed would deny the right of the individual to own property and would shift the protection of human rights from the control of those elected representatives of the people in legislative assemblies, to the hands of 5 judges appointed by the prime minister."

Campbell continued:

"We call on you, Mr. Prime Minister, and all our elected Parliamentarians, federal and provincial, who share with you the responsibility, under God, for seeking to renew Canada's constitution, to enshrine these principles of freedom in a made-in-Canada, patriated constitution:

The innate and infinite worth of every human being, from conception to eternity, as 'made in the image of God';

The fact of individual moral accountability as fundamental to human dignity, and as essential to the functioning of the institutions of a civilized, democratic society;

The family, (i.e. husband, wife, and/or children) is the basic cell of a free and responsible society, the most dynamic environment in which a child may be nurtured to creative adulthood;

The child is a member of the family, not a ward of the state;

The state has a God-given mandate to foster a social environment in which 'well-doing' is rewarded, and 'evil-doing' is punished.

There is no authority except that which God has established...

The ruler...is God's servant to do you good...and an agent of wrath to bring punishment on the wrongdoer (Romans 13:1-5)." [22]

Reverend Ron Marr of the *Christian Inquirer*

Ron Marr was an evangelical Minister who edited a newspaper, *The Christian Inquirer,* which was distributed throughout the evangelical churches. Reverend Marr wrote a prophetic article in the newspaper in March, 1981:

"When Prime Minister Trudeau introduced his constitutional package, a majority of Canadians supported it. By January 1981, only 22% were reported supporting it. What happened?

First. The Charter of Rights. Very few want a charter of rights entrenched in a new constitution – at least, without much longer, more detailed public scrutiny.

What is wrong with the proposed Charter of Rights? It does not give a proper place to God, the family or morality. It does not protect in perpetuity property rights, and the right to life from conception until natural death....It opens the door for the fulfillment of the wildest aspirations of militant feminists and homosexuals.

The Charter of Rights...becomes only the twisted tool of civil libertarians to accomplish their devious goals for societal change."

He continued:

"It is becoming increasingly obvious that the Charter will

serve well the purposes of the elitists, the globalists, the civil rights activists and the imperial aspirations of Pierre Elliott Trudeau.

If we want the courts and the bureaucrats dictating our lives – giving us only those freedoms that seem good to them – if we want God left out of our essential law – if we want to accept the deliberate rejection of protection of property rights, right-to-life and the supremacy of law and the family...- if we want to make our essential rights dependent on government, not God – if we want the will of the Canadian people and their provinces flouted – if we want the high-handed imposition of the basic law of our nation by an autocratic Prime Minister who has repeatedly demonstrated his disdain of the people and any other force that would limit his determination of our destiny – if we want the increasingly liberal courts to be empowered to overrule any and all legislation...if that is what we want – that is what we've got." [23]

That statement pretty well summed up what the evangelical churches thought of Trudeau and his Charter.

With this intense pressure from the pro-life movement, MPs from the three parties continued to raise concerns about the Charter in the House of Commons, but to no avail. Trudeau refused to listen.

Chapter 9

The Supreme Court decision and the passing of the Constitutional Resolution

On October 14, 1980, a few days after the introduction of the constitutional proposal in Parliament, the provinces of Manitoba, Newfoundland and Quebec, believing that Trudeau's decision to act unilaterally on the Constitutional Resolution was illegal, met in Toronto and announced that they would fight the resolution in the courts.

The Appeal Court in Manitoba had previously ruled that the unilateral patriation bill was constitutional. However, on March 31, 1981, the Supreme Court of Newfoundland declared that the Liberal resolution was illegal. This set the stage for an appeal to the Supreme Court of Canada.

Trudeau was then forced to await the decision of the Supreme Court of Canada before proceeding further with his unilateral resolution on the constitution.

On September 28, 1981, the Supreme Court ruled that the federal government could not proceed without substantial provincial approval. The court concluded by a majority of 7 to 2, that the Liberal unilateral patriation was legal but it went on to say, by a judgment of six to three, that though legal, it was not according to constitutional convention. The court said there had to be a **"substantial number"** of provinces agreeing with the federal government's constitutional proposal. (emphasis ours) [1]

It is significant that there were three dissenting judges in this decision who had concluded that Trudeau's unilateral resolution on the constitution was legal, despite its lack of provincial consent. The three judges were Mr. Justice William McIntyre, Chief Justice Bora Laskin and Mr. Justice Willard Estey.

Judge McIntyre acted entirely properly by rendering his decision on the legality of Trudeau's unilateral decision and then removing himself from the ensuing debate. Judges Bora Laskin and Willard Estey, on the other hand, in an appalling breach of ethics and lack of judicial propriety, threw themselves into openly lobbying for the Charter in London on Trudeau's behalf.[2]

It was not surprising that Bora Laskin would enter the political fray on behalf of Trudeau's Charter. Laskin owed Trudeau big time for his appointment in 1973 as Chief Justice of the Supreme Court. Laskin, a constitutional expert, was Dean of the University of Toronto Law School from where he was appointed to the Ontario Court of Appeal in 1965. He was appointed to the Supreme Court of Canada by Trudeau in 1970. Three years later, in 1973, Trudeau controversially appointed Laskin as Chief Justice over Mr. Justice Ronald Martland who had been on the court for 15 years and who by tradition should have been appointed Chief Justice. Trudeau in his plans for constitutional reform wanted to be certain that he would have judicial support for his actions. There is no doubt that Laskin and Trudeau shared a common perspective on the need for the court to monitor and act against the decisions made by Members of Parliament if necessary. They thought MPs were impressionable, uninformed and ignorant, and the elite, knowledgeable judges were better able to make decisions on human rights.

Trudeau admitted in his memoirs that this decision by the Supreme Court did place constraints on him.[3]

Also, Trudeau had plenty of other opposition to his proposed constitution. For example, some NDP MPs were against it. Four MPs, Lorne Nystrom, Simon de Jong, Doug Anguish and Stan Hovdebo opposed the constitution as did the Premier of Saskatchewan Allan Blakeney. Some 37% of delegates to the NDP party convention in Vancouver in May 1981 also opposed the proposed constitution.[4]

The Quebec government announced it was bitterly opposed to the imposition of the Charter which would impact Quebec's culturally protective language law providing French to be the official language of Quebec life.[5]

The Quebec Liberals, led by Claude Ryan, also demanded new constitutional talks.

Trudeau, however, refused to budge. Chrétien stated, on September 30, 1981, as noted in the *Toronto Sun*:

> *"The federal government, facing renewed struggle over its proposed charter of rights, will act on provincial proposals only if they amount to improvements to the document."*

A spokesman for Chrétien said later "there was no way" Chrétien would consider dropping the Charter from the federal package, adding that it would be "unfair" to women and minority groups who would gain protection under the Charter.

In London, negative reaction to the Canadian Constitution and Charter was increasing in the UK Parliament.

Campaign Life promotes rejection in London

As Trudeau moved to obtain British support for the Constitution being repatriated from London, Campaign Life became active in encouraging UK politicians to reject his requests.

On August 24, 1981, Gwen Landolt wrote Sir John A. Biggs-Davidson on the recommendation of Dr. Peggy Norris, a member of the executive of the World Federation of Doctors Who Respect Human Life. She wanted to know how the pro-life group could best spend their money to prevent the passage of the proposed Charter of Rights in the UK.

Landolt explained the situation to Biggs-Davidson. At that time, she said, the Supreme Court was deliberating the legality of the proposed Constitution. After its decision, at the end of September, the House would debate it for two days, then vote on it. The Liberals had 147 of the 282 seats, and all were required to vote for it. The NDP would also support it.

Landolt described the main concern of the pro-life groups:

"The pro-life movement strongly objects to the Charter since it excludes the right to life of the unborn child and because, very importantly, lawyers across Canada have advised us that the present wording of the Charter will probably allow the Supreme Court of Canada to strike down any future legislation passed by Parliament to protect unborn children. According to these lawyers, any doubt as to the implications of the Charter to the pro-life cause was removed on April 23, last, when an amendment to the Charter (now s.28) was passed which reads as follows:

Notwithstanding anything in the Charter, the rights and freedoms referred to in it are guaranteed equally to male and female persons.

The reason for pro-life concern lies in the fact that the courts in Canada have ruled that the term "person" is restricted to those individuals already born. Further, sections 7 and 15 of the Charter are almost identical to Amendments 9 and 14 of the American Constitution which the U.S. Supreme Court applied in 1973 to render the decision that a "right to privacy" contained in Amendments 9 and 14 included a right to abortion-on-demand. Given the Canadian courts' consistent refusal to recognize legal personhood of the unborn child, there is every reason to believe that Canadian courts when interpreting the Charter of Rights will follow the reasoning of the American Supreme Court to establish a similar right to abortion-on-demand."[6]

Others were encouraging members of Campaign Life to go to the UK to petition directly. Fr. Albert Lalonde, OMI wrote Landolt on August 31, 1981, saying he made contact with Margaret White, an official of the Society for the Protection of Unborn Children (SPUC) about Campaign Life going to the UK.[7]

MP Sir John A. Biggs-Davidson and MP Sir John Braine were contacted by Campaign Life on October 6, 1981 for advice as to how to present its views to the House of Commons and House of Lords. The letter stated:

"Although our major interest initially was the narrow but vitally important pro-life issue, it has now broadened considerably in view of Lord Kershaw's Foreign Affairs

Committee Report which recommended that there be a consensus by the provincial premiers and this position was also recently taken by the Supreme Court of Canada i.e. that the majority of the provinces must agree to the proposed constitutional reform."

Mrs. Landolt consulted with Professor John Finnis of Oxford, a lawyer and constitutional expert on the federal system, who was the legal adviser to PM Margaret Thatcher on constitutional matters, including Canada's constitutional resolution. Landolt wrote, on October 15, 1981:

"One of our greatest difficulties has been that very few Canadians are informed as to the enormous changes that are being advocated by the federal government. They for the most part believe that the change in the constitution will not have a direct effect on their lives. However, such is not the case." [8]

Professor Finnis, in his reply dated October 20, 1981 to Mrs. Landolt, advised her that the UK Parliament would not pass the Canadian proposal without the consent of the provinces.

Kay Cleverley wrote Campaign Life to let them know that Canadian provincial governments and aboriginal nations have all been lobbying in the UK.

"There is a danger that we shall be swamped and, indeed confused by some of the side issues, however important their advocates think they may be."

She recommended Campaign Life get in touch with the All Party Committee headed by Jonathan Aitken and George Foulkes. [9]

The lobbying efforts in the United Kingdom to oppose Trudeau's constitutional package had powerful results.

A letter dated October 29, 1981 was published in the *London Times*, in which 21 MPs rejected Trudeau's repatriation plans. The letter stated:

"These measures (Trudeau's constitution) have proven highly contentious within Canada and are strongly opposed by 8 of the 10 provincial governments whose consent is constitutionally required for amendments to the B.N.A. Act which affect their powers.

This view was upheld by the Supreme Court of Canada which

on September 28, 1981, stated that the Federal request to the United Kingdom Parliament 'without such (provincial) agreement would be unconstitutional in the conventional sense'.

We do not believe that the United Kingdom Parliament should be forced to enact unconstitutional legislation pursuant to a unilateral request from the Canadian federal government. While we do sincerely wish for a settlement that will quickly place the Canadian Constitution fully into Canadian hands there is no question in our minds that until a constitutionally appropriate request is made Parliament has no choice but to continue its residual role in the constitutional affairs of Canada."[10]

Despite the Liberals' public statements that it would proceed with the constitutional proposal regardless of the opposition to it, with the Supreme Court of Canada decision requiring that the majority of provinces approve the constitutional proposals, Trudeau had no choice but to meet yet again with the premiers to seek their approval. They met on November 5, 1981.

Trudeau manipulates provinces to get agreement

At this meeting, Trudeau cleverly divided the provinces which opposed his plans. He met first with Quebec's Lévesque and suggested to him that they just repatriate the Constitution and then have discussions later on an amending formula and the Charter of Rights. He said if there was no such agreement, a referendum could be held. René Lévesque agreed. [11]

Trudeau then returned to the other premiers who were objecting to his proposal, and said there was a Quebec-Ottawa alliance for a referendum. The seven premiers were furious with Lévesque, but this information (misleading as it was) did have the effect of the premiers starting serious discussions. The explosive situation was described by Robert Sheppard in *The Globe & Mail* on November 6, 1981:

"According to key insiders, the final straw that set up the deal and allowed the various provinces to abandon their Quebec ally came only after Premier René Lévesque of Quebec unexpectedly threw his support behind Prime Minister

Pierre Trudeau's casual suggestion to hold a referendum on the issue of the Charter of Rights.

None of the other premiers wanted a referendum and so Mr. Lévesque's solo move made it easier for the rest to meet the Prime Minister's bottom-line demand on language rights, ministers from several key provinces said...

(Trudeau) left those in the room with the impression that if they did not go along he would be making the offer (of a referendum) publicly to at least ease the concerns of British MPs."

The premiers did not want a referendum because they didn't like the optics of having to campaign against Trudeau's, often repeated, but incorrect, argument that he was expanding and enshrining rights under a Charter when they knew that Canadians already enjoyed such rights without a Charter.

At 9:30 a.m. on November 5, 1981, the premiers and officials from Alberta, Saskatchewan and Newfoundland met in Saskatchewan Premier Blakeney's suite at the Chateau Laurier Hotel to consider a two-page document that Premier Peckford of Newfoundland had drawn up. This included the option of including a notwithstanding clause in the Charter. Officials from PEI, Nova Scotia and BC later joined this meeting.

The *Toronto Star* reported that later that day, federal Justice Minister Chrétien, Saskatchewan Attorney General Romanow and Ontario Attorney General McMurtry met in the kitchen of the Convention Centre across the street from the Chateau Laurier, and agreed at that time to accept the Charter with a *notwithstanding clause*. This became known in popular myth as the "Kitchen Accord".[12]

Plamondon says something similar:

"Building upon ideas and a document that came from Newfoundland Premier Brian Peckford, representatives from Ontario and Saskatchewan met with Chrétien and accepted the Charter of Rights, with a notwithstanding clause, the 7/50 Alberta amending formula and no fiscal compensation for opting out.

Trudeau agreed to the deal after Davis called him...

> *Later Chrétien persuaded him to agree to fiscal compensation for opting out and giving Quebec control over immigrant minority education rights."* [13]

The heroes of this Accord, according to this popular myth then were Jean Chrétien, Roy Romanow and Roy McMurtry. This trio allegedly brought the agreement together. These three men have been dining out for years on their supposed constitutional breakthrough on that fateful November 5, 1981. They have happily accepted accolades for this alleged achievement over the ensuing years. As recently as December 10, 2012, they were recognized by the Institute on Governance in Ottawa for their supposed role in repatriating the Canadian Constitution and creating the Charter of Rights.

This latter award, however, was the last straw for an annoyed former Newfoundland Premier, Brian Peckford, who wrote to the President and Board of Directors of the Institute of Governance objecting to the award to Chrétien, Romanow and McMurtry. In his email dated March 20, 2013 addressed to the organization, Peckford, referred to his book published in September, 2012 entitled *"Some Day The Sun Will Shine and Have Not Will Be No More"* in which he described the so-called "Kitchen Accord" in quite a different light. He stated that it was a thirty-year-old myth that the trio had brought forward the constitutional proposal for settlement. Rather, he claimed that he and the Newfoundland delegation had played that significant role in coming up with the compromise agreement on the *notwithstanding clause*, and that this should be properly acknowledged.

The details of the Accord, according to Mr. Peckford, were that his proposal for a constitutional settlement was presented to the premiers at a critical breakfast meeting at the Chateau Laurier Hotel on November 5, 1981. Officials from British Columbia, Alberta and Saskatchewan were present and poured over his written proposal. Other premiers were then brought in. According to Mr. Peckford, this proposal by Newfoundland formed the basis of the final agreement. After some minor adjustments, the federal government, plus Ontario and New Brunswick agreed to sign on to this agreement.

Mr. Peckford's version of the events has been confirmed by

Carleton University political historian, Stephen Azzi, who has reviewed the documents covering that crucial Accord, and concluded that "Mr. Peckford and the Newfoundland delegation played the significant role, one which has to be acknowledged properly".[14]

Quebec excluded from federal-provincial agreement

Unfortunately, Premier Lévesque was not involved in the intense negotiations by the provinces that took place. He had retired to his hotel and he did not have any knowledge of the Accord until he returned to the conference the following morning when it was a *fait accompli*. Understandably, Levesque believed he had been betrayed by Trudeau and the nine premiers from the English speaking provinces. He left the conference deeply hurt and angered.

This federal-provincial agreement reached in the absence of Quebec left a deep wound within Quebec that has never healed. Consequently, the Charter has not become a part of Quebec's culture and life, but is always regarded as a governing instrument forced on them. This has only deepened Quebec's alienation from the rest of Canada to this day. Subsequent attempts to appease Quebec by way of Prime Minister Brian Mulroney's proposed *Meech Lake Agreement* and the *Charlottetown Accord*, both of which failed, only exacerbated the problem of Quebec's alienation.

The Notwithstanding Clause

The key to this federal-provincial agreement (with the exception of Quebec) was the addition of a Notwithstanding Clause. This clause covered sections dealing with Fundamental Freedoms, Legal Rights and Equality Rights. This clause (Section 33) of the charter provided that a federal or provincial government could place a decision of the Supreme Court of Canada on hold and proceed with the law notwithstanding the Supreme Court decision for a five-year period which could be renewed.[15]

Ontario's Bill Davis had insisted that Trudeau accept the Notwithstanding Clause. Trudeau stated Davis called him and said:

"Look Pierre, I think we have to tell you that this is a good compromise from our point of view. Rather than fight this thing to the bitter end, we have to tell you that we wouldn't

go to London supporting you as we have until now if you don't accept some sort of compromise of this nature. We can argue details tomorrow, but we like the outline of the compromise."[16]

Trudeau accepted it because he needed the agreement of the provincial premiers, and he knew opposition was mounting in England to his unilateral constitutional proposal.

Trudeau did demand that minority language rights be excluded from the notwithstanding formula.[17]

Later, Chrétien persuaded Trudeau to agree to fiscal compensation for opting out and giving Quebec control over immigrant minority education rights.[18]

Apparently, according to a fact sheet provided by the federal government for the notwithstanding clause, this was not a unique procedure in Canada's history:

"The notwithstanding principle has been recognized and is contained in a number of bills of rights, including the Canadian Bill of Rights (1960), the Alberta Bill of Rights (1972), the Quebec Charter of Rights and Freedoms (1975), the Saskatchewan Human Rights Code (1979), and Ontario's Bill 7 to Amend its Human Rights Code (1981)." [19]

The Progressive Conservative Party accepted the Accord with the notwithstanding clause.

However, Gordon Gilchrist (PC, Scarborough East) didn't agree with it at all. He summarized the Accord, in *The Globe and Mail* of December 3, 1981, as follows:

"It's not a constitution; it's a prostitution, an 11th hour, 55th minute mishmash thrown together by the premiers…He cited three objections – no protection for the unborn, no protection of Anglo-Quebecers, and no protection for property rights."

There is no doubt that at least one of the provincial premiers was well aware that the Charter would have a direct effect on the abortion issue, at least provincially. This was Alan Blakeney, premier of Saskatchewan. On the evening of November 5, 1981 when he was interviewed on the popular CBC radio programme "As it Happens", he mentioned the possibility that the Supreme Court of

Canada may interpret s.15 of the Charter so as to require hospitals to provide abortions. He stated that under such circumstances, the provincial government would have to determine whether it would then pass legislation "overriding" the court's decision.

Lawyers hated the inclusion of the notwithstanding clause in the Charter. Quebec historian Bastien writes:

"The ink on the final agreement wasn't yet dry, and already every lawyer in Canada was rushing to attack the cursed disposition. Law students were circulating petitions demanding its abrogation, supported by the Canadian Bar Association. The offensive was also supported by universities, notably by law faculties, which took a resolutely post-modern turn by sacralizing the Charter while damning Section 33." [20]

Chrétien thought the notwithstanding clause would not be important. Speaking in the House of Commons on November 20, 1981 he noted:

"What the premiers and the Prime Minister agreed to is a safety valve which is unlikely ever to be used except in non-controversial circumstances by Parliament or legislatures to override certain sections of the Charter. The purpose of an override clause is to provide the flexibility that is required to ensure that legislatures rather than judges have the final say on important matters of public policy." [21]

In his same speech, Chrétien quoted Allan Borovoy, general counsel to the Canadian Civil Liberties Association as saying, in the *Montreal Gazette* of November 7, 1981:

"Our reaction is one of great relief. They did not emasculate the charter...

The process is a rather ingenious marriage of a bill of rights nation and a parliamentary democracy. The result is a strong charter with an escape valve for the legislature. The "notwithstanding" clause will be a red flag for opposition parties and the press. That will make it politically difficult for a government to override the charter. Political difficulty is a reasonable safeguard for the charter."

Finally, Chrétien quoted Gordon Fairweather, Commissioner of the Canadian Human Rights Commission:

"I'm feeling tremendously upbeat...

The override clause will become as dead from lack of use as a clause in the British North America Act that, at least in theory, still enables Ottawa to disallow provincial legislation. Referring to long standing provincial opposition to entrenched rights, Mr. Fairweather said, 'The gang of no has become the gang of yes'."

It is interesting that Joe Clark, leader of the PCs, said in Commons also on November 20, 1981:

"We are a deliberative and legislative body, not a rubber stamp for a prime minister or for premiers. That obligation to act is most profound in fields where Parliament is the sole or crucial custodian of vital national interests, such as the state of our aboriginal people or the unity of our divided nation."[22]

Sadly, Clark would do exactly the opposite, leading the PCs to approve what the Prime Minister and premiers had negotiated.

Others among the Conservatives worried about the future with judges in control. MP Ray Hnatyshyn said on November 24, 1981:

"Canadians will be faced with a judiciary which will be obliged to exercise a quasi-legislative role in interpreting the new Charter of Rights and Freedoms. We will soon realize that the composition of the courts and the political and social beliefs of our judges will be an extremely important factor in the determination of the rights and prerogatives of citizens and institutions in the country. Indeed, the power of appointment of judges from time to time will be of immense importance in the ultimate determination and interpretation of fundamental rights in Canada. [23]

Last minute efforts to oppose the Constitution

The heads of Canadian Catholic universities signed a letter to *The Globe and Mail* November 5, 1981 protesting against the lack of protection for the unborn: St. Mark's College in Vancouver, St. Joseph's College in Edmonton, St. Paul's College in Winnipeg, St. Thomas More College in Saskatoon, St. Francis Xavier University in Antigonish, and St. Michael's College in Toronto joined together to state:

"The Charter of Rights, as it stands, really does present a grave and far-reaching danger to the very right which it claims to protect."

Campaign life also rejected the accord. In a newsletter dated Nov 10, 1981 Campaign Life stated:

"If this agreement becomes the constitution of Canada, it will cause incalculable and perhaps permanent damage to the pro-life cause in Canada."

It noted one benefit was the notwithstanding clause which would allow the opt out if the courts ruled for abortion on demand. However, they acknowledged the difficulty of implementing this, quoting Gordon Fairweather, an ardent pro-abortionist and former head of the New Brunswick Human Rights commission:

"the opting out clause will become ...dead from lack of use."

"The battle would be a never-ending one, as even if a province used it, they would be obliged to renew the battle every five years." [24]

On Nov 19, 1981 Kathleen Toth wrote all MPs asking them to oppose the Accord:

"We protest the sacrifice of the lives of our unborn in the name of women's liberation. Although sections on equality may be overridden, they will continue to jeopardize the lives of our young through abortion. This will happen unless an amendment is introduced in the Charter granting protection for life from conception onwards.

Failing this we call on all MPs who value the lives of the unborn to defeat the passage of this Charter, for it is a Charter of injustice."

Some MPs, including Joe Clark, Hazen Argue and Don Mazankowski confirmed they had received her letter and would be giving it full consideration, but then supported the Charter anyway. [25]

Prime Minister Trudeau rejected her proposal, saying that abortion was:

"an evolving moral and social issue. In view of this, the government's position is that the question of abortion should not be decided by the constitution."

161

On November 19, 1981 Gwen Landolt wrote to PC MP Douglas Roche:

> *"We continue to believe that "there is no protection for the unborn in the constitution, and that the result will lead to abortion on demand."* [26]

On November 25, 1981, Cardinal Carter, apparently having second thoughts about the Charter, made an appeal to have the unborn protected in a telegram to Trudeau in which he stated:

> *"As indicated in my earlier correspondence and that of Archbishop MacNeil of Edmonton, former President of the Canadian Conference of Catholic Bishops, with whom I have consulted, I in company with millions of Canadians of all religions, am distressed by the present failure of the proposed charter of rights to protect in any way the rights of our unborn children. I suggest one of two courses: either a statement that nothing in the charter may be interpreted as infringing on these rights, or at the very least a statement that notwithstanding any provision in the charter, parliament shall not be precluded from legislating the rights of unborn children."* [27]

Kathleen Toth wrote in praise of Cardinal Carter's letter:

> *"The significance of the Cardinal Carter telegram is mainly that the Roman Catholic hierarchy of Canada now concurs that there is a reasonable doubt that the Charter is not neutral concerning the rights of the unborn children. There is a clear danger that the Supreme Court will be able to use various sections of the Charter to strike down laws of Parliament to protect unborn children."* [28]

Gwen Landolt was more resigned. She wrote that:

> *"... at that point in time, however, Mr. Trudeau concluded that he did not need the support of the Church and totally ignored its request."* [29]

Resolution respecting Constitution Act, 1981

On November 26, 1981, Jean Chrétien tabled the amended motion on a resolution respecting the Constitution Act, 1981. [30]

On November 26, 1981 David Crombie proposed his amendment to protect the abortion issue from the judges' oversight. As we read previously, it was defeated.

John Stephens, commenting on the vote said:

"All the politicians were off the hook – the Liberals because they stuck to their point of neutrality, the Tories because it got to a vote." [31]

Constitution approved

Pressure was intense on all MPs to support the Constitution. Very few pro-life MPs had the courage to follow their beliefs.

One was Liberal MP Garnet M. Bloomfield. In a statement to MPs on Nov 20, 1981 Mr. Bloomfield said the following:

"First of all I would like to say that I support the proposal of bringing the constitution home to Canada with an amending formula, the charter of rights also contains many principles that I agree with but it has one very serious fault or omission in that there is no protection for the unborn, no right to life clause. How can we as a society give protection to the many other groups such as the handicapped and the disabled and deny the right to life of the most defenseless of the human family, the unborn.

I am also very concerned about the legal tangle that could ensue over whether an unborn child is an individual before birth.

I not only worry about the unborn not being protected in the charter but also their future plight quite possibly left in the hands of the supreme court because of the equivocal language employed in the proposed charter of rights." [32]

Another Liberal was Stanley Hudecki (Hamilton West). He stated his reasons for doing so were as follows:

"My vote against the proposed constitution was a protest vote. I am protesting failure of the Charter to give any added protection to the unborn and the distinct possibility that it will weaken the protection afforded by the Criminal Code of Canada...

When the Constitution Act is proclaimed with the present

sections of the Charter entrenched, four clauses in the Act will deal prominently with abortion laws in the future. These clauses present ambiguities and will require interpretation by the Supreme Court of Canada to clarify their meaning...

Section 7 the word 'liberty' can be interpreted by judges to mean privacy of person and consequently it could be construed as it was in the Supreme Court of the United states that a woman has the right to privacy. A pregnancy interferes with that privacy. It could be interpreted that to refuse such a woman an abortion interferes with the right to privacy and it could be argued that she therefore has legal rights to abortion on demand circumventing the provision of the Criminal Code.

Under section 15 a woman can demand equal benefit of the law. This could be interpreted that in areas where hospitals do not provide abortion facilities, court action could be instituted on the basis of discrimination against women forcing local hospitals to provide abortion facilities or forcing the Ministers of Health for the provinces to set up abortion facilities...

Clause 28 of Section 33 reinforces the rights of equality to male and female persons regardless of anything previously said in the charter...This could ... force all hospitals receiving public funds to provide abortion facilities." [33]

Voting against the Liberal constitutional resolution were five Liberals, including Warren Allmand, Jean Robert Gauthier, Louis Duclos, Garnet Bloomfield and Stan Hudecki, 17 Conservatives: Thomas Cossitt, Elmer MacKay, Ronald Huntington, Roch LaSalle, Alex Patterson, Gordon Towers, Doug Roche, Frank Cherle, Doug Neil, Gus Mitges, Dan McKenzie, Otto Jelinek, Len Gustafson, Gordon Gilchrist, John Gamble, Bill Domm and Ron Stewart and two NDP MPs: James Manley and Svend Robinson. Robert Ogle abstained.

Commenting on the vote, Jean Morse-Chevrier, of Ottawa Pro-life, said:

"Only seven members of the House of Commons voted against the charter for pro-life reasons (although we do have 85 allegedly pro-life members). A total of 24 from all par-

ties voted against it for other reasons. If party discipline had not been so strong we may perhaps have got the amendment through."[34]

According to *The Globe & Mail*, of December 3, 1981:

"Jake Epp is being credited with keeping the number of dissidents down to 17."

Earlier that day it was rumoured 45 would vote against it.

The Senate approves the Constitution

Once the Constitution proposal had passed the House of Commons on December 2, 1981, it was merely a formality that the Liberal majority in the Senate would pass it.

Campaign Life literally leaving no stone unturned, wrote to the Senate nonetheless, to raise their concerns once again about the Charter's effect on the abortion issue. In a letter to each Senator, dated December 4, 1981 Campaign Life asked them to amend the Constitution by providing protection for the unborn child.[35]

Senator Joseph Sullivan introduced an amendment, seconded by John MacDonald, on December 4 stating everyone – including the unborn child – has the right to life. They and 26 other senators voted for it, while 50 voted against it. A second resolution was then introduced stating "everyone has the right to life from the moment of conception onwards". This motion was defeated 16 to 50.[36]

Trudeau obviously was not concerned that the Liberal-dominated Senate would not pass his Constitutional Resolution but he took no chances. He appointed Senator Ray Perrault as the Senate's House Leader. Senator Perrault was a well-known pro-life Catholic, (a popular president of the Catholic Newman Club while a student at UBC). Another prominent longtime Liberal Senator, at that time, was Senator John Connolly of Nova Scotia, who was also known as a pro-life Catholic. When Senator Connolly was questioned about the Charter's possible effect on abortion, he dismissed off-hand these concerns stating: "That won't happen".

It would be easy to dismiss the pro-life Liberal senators' and MPs' support for the Charter as being individuals who had put their party's concerns above their faith. This, however, would be too simple a response. Trudeau, by that time, had effectively sewed up the Charter debate relating to the abortion issue. He had both the

Catholic bishops and Cardinal Carter onside, the Liberal caucus supporting it, (with two notable exceptions, MP's Garnet Bloomfield and Dr. Stan Hudecki) and a string of legal opinions from the Department of Justice lawyers that the abortion law would not be affected by the Charter. This latter theme was constantly repeated and had become conventional wisdom by the time the resolution was brought before the Parliament. The Catholic MPs and senators therefore dismissed the concerns raised by Campaign Life as being without legal merit. If only that had been the case.

It seems the claim that abortion would not be affected by the Charter was taken as a self-evident truth.

Constitution Act proclaimed

On April 17, 1982, the Constitution Act of 1982 was proclaimed.

It was a hollow victory. No one celebrates the Constitution.

Plamondon writes:

> *"The new Constitution Act, proclaimed into law by Queen Elizabeth II on April 17, 1982, was not greeted with a day of national celebration, certainly not in Quebec. And it received no commemorations on its twentieth or thirtieth anniversaries either. If a Constitution is intended to unify the country, then Trudeau's document failed to pass this test."*

Elsewhere he notes:

> *"...while the Charter was arguably designed to confer voices to the previously voiceless, Canadians never had the chance to pronounce directly on it themselves, either in an election, as they did with the Free Trade deal in 1988, or in a referendum, as they did with the Charlottetown Accord in 1993. While former Supreme Court Justice Frank Iacobucci observed that '[o]ur Charter's introduction and consequential remedial role of the courts were choices of the Canadian people through their elected representatives, as part of the redefinition of our democracy,' this statement holds true only at the highest level. Yes, we did elect a government, and a Prime Minister, that created the Charter. Yes, a host of interest groups and individuals were invited to weigh in on what they thought should go into the document. But Canadians*

were never consulted on the basic question of whether they wanted a charter or not. Had Trudeau done so, either at the ballot box or in a referendum, the Charter, had it passed such a test, might have made a real contribution to Canadian unity over the long term." [(37)]

Effectively, ten men (Mr. Trudeau and the premiers of the nine English-speaking provinces) had imposed a completely new constitution on Canadians. It was passed in the House of Commons and Senate. The Canadian Constitution, in fact, is the only one in the world which was drafted by way of telex and telephone calls and personal agreement by the parties involved, even though its impact on our country was monumental. In effect, it was carried out through a bloodless revolution.[(38)]

The deadly Poker play

The cards dealt to the adversaries in the deadly game of poker between Trudeau and the pro-life movement over the Charter, and the life of the unborn child, were not evenly matched.

The cards dealt the pro-life movement consisted of the implacable knowledge that the acceptance of the Charter would result in unrestricted abortion, and also the destruction of the nation's accepted moral and legal standards by way of nine unaccountable appointed judges on the Supreme Court of Canada. The pro-life movement had little money to promote its concerns. Its only real strength was a small army of volunteers from across the country. All of the volunteers knew, to the very core of their being, that the acceptance of the Charter would lead to the destruction of generations of helpless unborn children whose existence could be terminated easily for the convenience of others. This knowledge drove the pro-life movement with extraordinary courage and determination. No effort or demand made on the volunteers was too much. Picketers with their signs opposing the Charter met the Prime Minister and the premiers whenever they met. Thousands of pamphlets were distributed entitled "Did You Know", which outlined the implications of the entrenched Charter. There was feverish fundraising and constant lobbying, by letters and telephone calls to the MPs and premiers and to the editors of newspapers. These activities were non-stop during the Charter debate.

The few cards at the disposal of the pro-life movement were used intelligently and efficiently.

Trudeau had been dealt powerful cards which he used with cunning and skill. Most significantly, he had the levers of power at his disposal, a subdued cabinet, a majority of seats in Parliament, the public service at his disposal, including the acquiescent lawyers in the Department of Justice. He also had unlimited funds both to advertise his perspective and to carry out polling during sensitive periods during the negotiations.

The play was played out to the end tenaciously by both sides. Its ending was, perhaps, inevitable. In its newsletter dated November 10, 1981, Campaign Life summed up the epic battle as follows:

> *"We must walk this last lonely mile and fight this constitutional agreement to the end. When the history of this constitution struggle is written, at least it will be said that the pro-life movement in Canada was awake while most other Canadians slept; that we were one of the very few groups who readily understood the issue, who participated in it with all the moral and legal might that we could muster. We discussed; we wrote; we telegraphed; and we picketed. We could do no more and we must keep on fighting to the end."* [39]

Chapter 10

The fatal Supreme Court decision on abortion

Regina v. Morgentaler

On January 28, 1988, the Supreme Court of Canada struck down the 1969 abortion law in *Regina v. Morgentaler.*

The decision did **not** provide a constitutional right to abortion. Rather, the court stated that Parliament had jurisdiction to pass a law on abortion if it wished later to provide protection for the life of the unborn child.

The court did hold, however, that the abortion amendment, passed by Trudeau in 1969, was unconstitutional because it failed to provide equal access to abortion, contrary to S.7 of the Charter. What the Supreme Court of Canada actually decided in the *Morgentaler* case was that the abortion law was unacceptable on procedural grounds in that it contravened S. 7 of the Charter, which provides that:

Everyone has the right to life, liberty and security of the person and the right not to be deprived thereof, except in accordance with the principles of fundamental justice.

There is a significant fact about the Supreme Court of Canada's 1988 decision in the Morgentaler case that calls into question that decision.

Improper admission of evidence in the *Morgentaler* case

Four of the judges, Dickson, Beetz, Estey and Lamer, who supported striking down the abortion law, relied on a document to do so prepared by a pro-abortion physician and activist, Dr. Marion Powell, a member of *Doctors to Repeal the Abortion Law*. She had been commissioned in 1986 by the Ontario Liberal government to review the application of the abortion law in Ontario. In her report, for which she relied mainly on pro-abortion reference sources and authorities, she concluded that women did not have equal access to abortion in the province. This was the reason given by four Supreme Court judges for striking down the abortion law.

The "Powell Report", however, was tabled in the Ontario provincial legislature on January 29, 1987. The arguments in the *Morgentaler* case were heard three months previously, from October 7-10, 1986. A search of the Supreme Court's dockets in the *Morgentaler* case at the Supreme Court Registry indicated that no Notice of Motion to admit the Powell Report in evidence had been filed; i.e: it was not part of the court record. Therefore, the "Powell Report" was used as evidence, even though it was not in existence at the time the case was argued, and its existence as evidence was unknown to the opposing counsel, who, therefore, had no opportunity to cross-examine on the document as to its credibility.

The use of such evidence in this manner was unprecedented in the procedural rules of the court. Mr. Justice William McIntyre, one of the two dissenting judges on the Supreme Court of Canada in this case, objected to the reliance on such material by the other judges, and stated that the court should "place principal reliance upon the evidence given under oath in court" which was not the case in this decision of four of the judges striking down the abortion law.

Toronto Right to Life laid a complaint with the Canadian Judicial Council (CJC) on February 2, 1989 about this improper use of evidence, with the full knowledge, acquired through experience with the Judicial Council, that it would quickly dismiss the complaint. This it promptly did.

The real purpose for making the complaint to the CJC was to create a paper trail of factual information for future litigation on the abortion issue in order to point out that in the *Morgentaler* decision, four of the five majority judges improperly admitted evidence upon which they relied in reaching their decisions to strike down the abortion law.

The decision in *Morgentaler* was improperly decided. The effect of this decision was to wipe out any prohibitions, under any circumstances, of abortion so it became an unrestricted procedure. As a result of this, the pro-abortionists and feminists no longer needed the tools given them under the Charter to challenge any restrictions on abortion.

Chapter 11

Cardinal Carter tries to rectify the abortion situation

When the Supreme Court of Canada struck down the abortion law in the *Morgentaler* case, it stated in its judgment that the protection of the unborn child was a valid purpose of legislation. It called upon Parliament to pass legislation to provide a balance between the competing interests of the mother and the unborn child.

Scarcely a month after the *Morgentaler* decision, Cardinal Carter wrote a strongly worded letter to Prime Minister Brian Mulroney requesting that his government immediately act to pass an abortion law to correct the intolerable situation created by the striking down of the previous law. His letter was endorsed by the Pentecostal Assemblies of Canada, Alliance for Life, Right to Life Toronto, Campaign Life, the Ontario Conference of Catholic Bishops, the Knights of Columbus and the Catholic Women's League.[1]

On September 19, 1989, Cardinal Carter again wrote to Prime Minister Mulroney requesting that a law on abortion be introduced in Parliament reminding him that such a law could be drafted which would be constitutionally valid. Cardinal Carter warned in his letter, however, that the gestational approach to abortion would not be acceptable, and that a large number of elected legislators would not support a gestational approach to any new abortion law.

On November 3, 1989, Minister of Justice, Kim Campbell, introduced the Conservative bill on abortion, Bill C-43. The bill was a huge disappointment to the pro-life movement. Although the Supreme Court in the *Morgentaler* decision had directed Parliament to provide a balance between the interests of the mother and the unborn child, Bill C-43 provided no such balance. The bill, in fact, made no reference to the unborn child. It provided only legal protection for physicians who performed abortions for *health* reasons, which was defined so broadly so as to include physical, mental and psychological health.

In her statement on October 29, 1990 before the Senate Legal and Constitutional Committee, Ms. Campbell stated:

> *"In forming this opinion, the doctor would be able to take into consideration such factors as rape, incest, genetic defects and socio-economic factors."*

> *"That in regard to a woman's health, a doctor would consider all of the consequences of failure to induce an abortion* ... **for example social factors and personal aspirations** ...*"* (emphasis ours)

Bill C-43 provided that the doctor who approves the abortion "must be of the opinion" that the pregnancy is "likely to threaten" the pregnant woman's health. Because it would be all but impossible to prove that a physician did *not* form such an opinion, this proposed law was clearly unenforceable.

Justice Minister Campbell admitted that the law was unenforceable during her appearance before the Senate Legal and Constitutional Affairs Committee on October 29, 1990 when she stated at p.6 of her brief:

> *"As long as the opinion formed by the doctor who directs or performs the abortion is professionally formed and honestly held, it is* **basically unassailable**. (emphasis ours)

Ms. Campbell further reaffirmed the unenforceability of the law in a letter of the same date to physicians when she stated at p. 3:

> *"The legislation is designed to protect a doctor from being convicted under the new law..."*[2]

Under Bill C-43, abortions would be legal throughout the nine months of pregnancy. Also, the bill did not specify who could perform the abortion. It merely provided that abortion be carried out "under the direction of a medical practitioner". Consequently, nurses and technicians would have been permitted to perform abortions under this Bill if directed by a physician. Further, there was no provision in the Bill that the abortions be performed in hospitals. Consequently, abortion clinics could be established across the country to provide this service. Finally, there was no minimum age provided for an abortion to be performed.

In short, Bill C-43 was a completely inadequate abortion law. This created a dilemma for the pro-life movement.

Since Bill C-43 provided no protection for the unborn child, and in fact, facilitated the performance of an abortion, with the abortionist being given an unfettered authority to do so, the pro-life movement decided to reject the bill: it requested that Bill C-43 be withdrawn and that a new, more acceptable bill be introduced in Parliament to replace it.

The decision to reject Bill C-43 by the pro-life movement was a disappointment to the Canadian Conference of Catholic Bishops (CCCB). Bishop Robert Lebel, President of the CCCB stated … While 'seriously flawed,' C-43 would have been better than a "legislative vacuum" and would have confirmed that abortion is a matter of public morality and a criminal offence. [3]

That was the dilemma. Was it better to reject Bill C-43 in the expectation that a stronger law would replace it, or was it preferable to accept the deeply flawed bill that at least would have returned the abortion law to the Criminal Code as a matter of signalling the importance of the issue and public morality?

Despite the fact that Bill C-43 did not have the support of the pro-life movement, it passed the House of Commons on May 29, 1990, on a free vote that was very close, 140 to 131. When Bill C-43 was voted on in the Senate on January 31, 1991, however, there was a tied vote. The tied vote was provided by feminist B.C. Senator Pat Carney, who, although ill at the time, put in an appearance in the Senate to specifically defeat the bill. Under the Senate rules, a tied vote defeats the legislation. Bill C-43 was the first government bill to be defeated in the Senate in 30 years.

Contrary to the hopes of the pro-life movement, no government has attempted to introduce another abortion law since Bill C-43 was defeated. As a result, Canada remains one of the three countries in the world, with North Korea and China, that does not provide any protection for the unborn child.

Conclusion

The journey for life continues

Even during the stressful and intense struggle carried out by the pro-life movement during the Charter debates, it still carried on its pro-life efforts in other areas.

It faced considerable difficulties due to the circumstances that were unique to Canada, in that, under the Canadian parliamentary system that has evolved since Pierre Trudeau was Prime Minister, the Prime Minister's office (PMO) has acquired enormously increased, if not, dictatorial powers. As a result, the role of the Cabinet and Parliament itself has greatly diminished in influence. For example, the Prime Minister now controls who will be nominated as a candidate in his party. Consequently, a pro-life individual has great difficulty obtaining a nomination. This is especially the situation under Prime Minister Justin Trudeau who has explicitly stated that no pro-life candidate may obtain a nomination in his party. As a result, a private member's bill on abortion has difficulty making its way through Parliament. The PMO ruthlessly shuts down debate before it can reach even second reading, no matter how reasonable the bill, or how incremental it is, on the abortion issue.

Religious leadership has been weak in Canada since it has not stood up with any vigor and force and effect when pro-abortion

177

bills have been introduced. An example of this, as previously discussed, was in 1969 when Prime Minister Trudeau introduced an amendment to the abortion law which has resulted in the death of millions of unborn babies. Religious opposition to this amendment was muted at best.

Despite intense pro-life efforts, the Catholic bishops, as outlined in this book, supported the Charter of Rights which led to the Supreme Court striking down the abortion law, even as flawed as it was.

Despite these disappointments, the pro-life movement carried on. One important action taken, for example, occurred at Surrey Memorial Hospital in BC where pro-lifers gained control of the hospital board and stopped all abortions. It was the first time in Canada that the board of a major community hospital had gone against the will of its doctors by disbanding a functioning abortion committee. Another group similarly took control of the Victoria General Hospital.

NDP justice critic Svend Robinson (NDP, Burnaby) called on the government to prevent pro-life groups from gaining control of hospitals. He claimed women would resort to illegal abortions if they could not get legal ones. The BC Federation of Labour backed him. [1]

The Globe & Mail, on October 9, 1980, commented that the abolition of the therapeutic abortion committee by the pro-life majority:

> *"...is only the visible crest of a controversy that has been building for several years in the Vancouver area and which its participants claim will have repercussions all across the country."*

Kathleen Toth, of Campaign Life responded by saying:

> *"...it is perhaps the only argument that the pro-abortionist use to justify the ruthless killing of unborn children that has any major impact on the public. As a result of this, it is absolutely crucial that Pro-Life must at every opportunity, counter this argument with the facts."*

Campaign Life then offered some statistics to all MPs. Before the abortion amendment in 1969, from 1965 to 1969, only 39 women died in abortions. Then, after it was legal, from 1970 to 1978, 31 died. There has been a minimal reduction in maternal deaths, but 450,000 children have died from 1970 to 1978 from abortions.[2]

In November 1980, the Catholic Women's League of Canada submitted a brief to Trudeau and Chrétien. They noted they were formed in 1923 and were concerned with upholding Christian values in the public and private sectors. They represented over 116,000 women. The brief presented the CWL position on eight major issues. One of these was education and they asked that the Constitution preserve the "rights of parents to denominational schools as presently enshrined in the B.N.A. Act, Section 93". On family life, they urged the government to be "vigilant in recognizing the need for legal protection of the unborn and the value of human life until the time of natural birth".

In the appendix to its brief, the Catholic Women's League attached its 1976 statement on the right to life, a basic norm of society, as well as its 1979 statement on human rights, which reaffirmed the sanctity of life of the unborn child.

It followed this up by encouraging its councils in the individual Catholic parishes to fund pro-life initiatives. On Dec 1, 1980, the national president of the Catholic Women's League sent a letter to local presidents informing them of a pro-life initiative with the Coalition for the Protection of Human Life. She stated:

> "You will find included in this mailing a letter to the Presidents of the CWL in all Canadian Parishes from the Coalition for the Protection of Human Life. This organization is the political arm of the Alliance for Life and has been working steadily to gain equal protection of the law for every human being, from the time of conception through all the stages of life, by lobbying all levels of government because, like us, Coalition is not a charitable organization and donations to it are not tax exempt. On this account, it is technically cut off from many potential sources of funding and as such, is badly in need of outside financial support." [3]

The *Manitoba Pro-Life News* magazine, in November 1980, called on members to "express your view that the proposed Charter of Human Rights should include the right to life for all Canadians, born or unborn". It asked members to write Pierre Trudeau, Jean Chrétien and Manitoba Premier Sterling Lyon.

This was a fairly active group and included the Manitoba Pro-Life Movement, the League for Life of Manitoba and the Winnipeg League for Life. In 1980, they organized a walkathon in Dauphin, La Broquerie, Roblin, St. Malo, Ste. Rose and Winnipeg. They were supported by the Knights of Columbus. There were 14 pro-life groups in Manitoba at that time.[4]

In Quebec, Msgr. Adolphe Proulx, Bishop of Hull, asked Sacre-Coeur Hospital in Hull to change its name to Centre Hospitalier Régionale de l'Outaouais. He made the request in response to the large number of abortions being performed at the hospital. He judged that the Christian name was no longer appropriate.[5]

Legal Interventions

A few weeks after the Supreme Court of Canada handed down its decision on the Morgentaler case in January 1988, the seven dockets of the case were reviewed in the office of the Registrar of the Supreme Court. The contents of the dockets showed that there was not one single pro-life document included in the dockets. All the information and evidence was pro-abortion.

It was apparent that such a situation should never be allowed to occur again in pro-life pro family legal challenges.

Abortion cases quickly arose in the courts but unfortunately there were no organizations available, either willing or able, other than REAL Women of Canada, to intervene in these cases. REAL Women is a pro-life/family organization of women federally incorporated in 1983. Consequently REAL Women took on the financial and legal responsibility to intervene in the series of abortion cases that quickly followed on the heels of the Morgentaler decision. REAL Women's legal counsel in these cases was Toronto lawyer Angela Costigan. Angela had previously argued a high profile case, *Murphy v. Dodd* in 1989, in which a putative father attempted to prevent his girlfriend from having an abortion. Angela argued the following cases on the abortion issue before the Supreme Court of Canada on behalf of REAL Women of Canada: *Borowski v. Canada* (1989); *Tremblay v. Daigle* (1989); *R. v. Sullivan and Lemay* (1991); and *R. v. Morgentaler* (1993). Angela was also legal counsel in the Supreme Court of Canada on behalf the pro-life education umbrella group Alliance for Life in *Winnipeg Child and Family Services v. D.F. G.* (1997).

In all these cases the radical feminist group, Women's Legal Education and Action Fund (LEAF), also intervened. It rapidly became apparent in all these cases that the Supreme Court of Canada was only interested in the "progressive" approach to the abortion issue. The sanctity of life arguments put forward by REAL Women and Alliance for Life were of little consequence to the court. This was the situation despite the fact that LEAF's factums frequently read like a feminist screed, with little legal arguments included in it.

No doubt LEAF had realized, as did REAL Women, that the "progressive" courts were not going to listen to REAL Women, and instead, regarded LEAF as the only authentic voice of women on the abortion issue in Canada. This was evidenced by the fact that seldom were LEAF's arguments rejected by the courts in its legal challenges over the years.

REAL Women, however, persisted in intervening in the courts despite the fact it did not enjoy the advantages of LEAF, which was being federally funded by the Court Challenges Program for its legal expenses, as well having its operational expenses funded by the Status of Women.

REAL Women continued to intervene in the courts because it wanted to establish, for the record, that women's views were not uniform, and many women did not support LEAF's pro-abortion position. Also, very importantly, REAL Women wished to prevent judges in later years from exonerating themselves from their many extraordinary decisions (based not on legal merit but rather, on their own personal ideology or bias) because they had no choice but to do so since no contrary arguments had been placed before them. There were contrary arguments by REAL Women presented before the courts, well thought out, legally based arguments, which the liberal judges chose to ignore in their pursuit of changing Canada's social values to a liberal perspective.

Fortunately today, there are a number of outstanding organizations that are intervening in the courts on behalf of the sanctity of life, family, religious liberty and parental rights. Some of these are: Evangelical Fellowship of Canada (EFC), Catholic

Civil Rights League (CCRL), Faith and Freedom Alliance (FFA), Christian Legal Fellowship (CLF), Association for Reformed Political Action (ARPA), the Justice Centre for Constitutional Freedoms (JCCF), the Home School Legal Defense Association of Canada (HSLDA), the Euthanasia Prevention Coalition (EPC), and the Canadian Council of Christian Charities (CCCC) to name a few. These organizations and others are providing outstanding, even brilliant, legal arguments before the courts by their lawyers. The latter are André Schutten (APRA), Philip Horgan (CCRL and FFA), Don Hutchinson and Faye Sonier (EFC), Robert Reynolds, Gerald Chipeur Q.C., Ruth and Derek Ross, Geoffrey Cowper, Philip Fourie, Deina Warren (CLF), John Carpay (JCCF) Paul Faris (HSLDA), Barry Bussey (CCCC), and Hugh Scher (EPC). Other lawyers or advocates involved in these critical issues today making outstanding legal contributions are: Robert Staley, Kevin Boonstra, Albertos Polizogopoulos, Dr. Charles Lugosi, Gwendoline Allison, Janet Epp Buckingham, Iain Benson, and others, whose contributions are outstanding on so many worthwhile issues.

Pro-life Resolve

One would assume that the losses experienced by the pro-life movement in the latter part of the 20th century shattered its resolve and caused despair, leading to the crumbling of its will. This did not happen.

The pro-life movement has moved on into the twenty-first century, building a culture of life by using the technological advances of the Internet, Facebook, Twitter and YouTube. In 1997, LifeSite News was established, which is an international internet service and powerful resource for culture, life and family issues. Its website serves as a portal for news reports and information, averaging 4-5 million visitors a month.

Pro-life projects continue to keep the issue alive. The annual *National March for Life* in Ottawa, organized by Campaign Life, attracts many thousands. A pro-life organization called *We Need a Law* planted 100,000 blue and pink flags (to represent the approximate number of abortions in Canada per year) on Parliament Hill on October 2, 2014, and later on the grounds of provincial legislatures. Pro-life MPs continue regularly to introduce pro-life bills and petitions in the House of Commons.

Young pro-life men and women are currently in training on university campuses across the country, pitting themselves against university administrators from another generation, who are grimly holding on to the *status quo*. The pro-life struggle on campuses is also pitted against the ideologically-based student unions, which also want to maintain the *status quo* by stamping out any alternative to unrestricted abortion.

The pro-life movement, in effect, has remained intact, preparing for the future. What has changed are the individuals now assuming roles of responsibility within the pro-life network. These young men and women are a different breed of pro-life leaders.

The first pro-life leaders were (and still are) passionate and angry at the injustice caused to the unborn. These individuals were called together from cities, hamlets and villages across the country because they had heard the cries of the helpless unborn child. They were unable to ignore them. These first pro-life leaders put aside their regular lives, in an unwelcoming world, to respond to the defense of the unborn child. They had no map to follow; they faced ridicule even among friends and family for their failure to be progressive in the modern world, and surmounted huge hurdles along their path placed there by the media and the government. Nonetheless, they persevered, knowing to the very core of their being that something had to be done. They were willing to take up this tremendous challenge, no matter the personal cost to themselves or condescension from others. These pro-life leaders could not betray their conscience on this central issue of the dignity of human life. No struggle was too difficult, no river too deep to cross or no road too long to travel. It had to be done.

The new breed of pro-life leaders is different in that they are cooler, implacable, and make their moves with shrewd calculation. They have been raised in a different era with new technical advances. They use the latest communication techniques to carry on the cause.

During the pro-life battle in the future there will be another difference. In the past struggles, the tidal wave has been against pro-life efforts which have caused pro-life efforts to be swept aside. The tidal wave in the future will be moving with the pro-life direction as is presently occurring in the US.

The prayerful, optimistic view of Jim Hughes, President of Campaign Life, a warrior present from the beginning, gives the proper perspective for the future:

When I consider the future of the pro-life movement, I am fondly reminded of Fr. Richard John Neuhaus who accepted our invitation to speak at a Campaign Life conference in 2002. In his remarks he welcomed all the young people and he said "It's great to see all the young people involved here, but you older people are here for the duration. You're here to mentor to the young people so they don't make the same mistakes you made." *Today, I hear the strong echo of Fr. Neuhaus as I read the wise and encouraging words of Cardinal George Pell of Australia:* "The role of young people is to set the world on fire. The role of old people is to make sure you don't burn the place down!"[6]

Endnotes

Chapter 1

1. Fr Alphonse de Valk, CSB, *Morality and Law in Canadian Politics – The Abortion Controversy*, (Montreal: Palm Publishers, 1974), pp.1, 4-5. All information and quotes for this section are found in these pages.

2. *Ibid*, pp.5-7 for this section.

3. *Ibid*, pp.10-26 is the source for this section. Additional references note which sources Fr. de Valk quoted. Rev. Ray Goodall, "Is Abortion ever Right", *Chatelaine*, March 1963, pp.40 & 48; Rev. Ray Goodall, "A Case for Induced Abortion", May 1963, United Church *Observer*, pp.15-6.

4. Proceedings Canadian Bar Association, 1966, p.91. De Valk, *Morality*, pp.23-4.

5. Proceedings Canadian Bar Association, 1966, p.102.

6. Report of the Special Committee on Therapeutic Abortions and Sterilizations, Ontario Medical Association, May 1965, p.1; the article by Gerald Waring is in *C.M.A.J.*, vol.97, November 11, 1967, 1233; De Valk, *Morality*, pp.17-9.

7. De Valk, *Morality*, pp.21-2

8. Letter, Paul Formby to Pope John Paul II, November 10, 1981 notes the percentage of Catholics in Canada. https://en.wikipedia.org/wiki/Catholicism_in_Canada notes the percentage of Catholics in 2001 as 43.6%; http://www.pewforum.org/2013/06/27/canadas-changing-religious-landscape/ notes it at 47% in 1971.

9. This section is based on *The Vatican II Revolution 1962-1965* chapter 8, available at http://www.mostholyfamilymonastery.com/8_ VaticanII.pdf, entitled *The Heresies of Vatican II.*; *Decrees of the Ecumenical Councils*, Vol. 2, p. 914; Denzinger, *The Sources of Catholic Dogma*, B. Herder Book. Co., Thirtieth Edition, 1957, no. 1777, 1755, 1690; *Decrees of the Ecumenical Councils*, Vol. 2, p. 1002; Benedict XVI, *Principles of Catholic Theology*, San Francisco, CA: Ignatius Press, 1982, p. 381, 385, 391; *The Papal Encyclicals*, Vol. 2 (1878-1903), pp. 175-176; *Decrees of the Ecumenical Councils*, Vol. 2, p. 1105, 1085, 1132; Msgr Foy, *Is there a Positive Side to the Winnipeg Statement*, available at www.msgrfoy.com; Michael Davies: Defender of the Faith or Faithless Heretic, Br. M. Dimond, http://www.mostholyfamilymonastery; Pope Benedict XVI, interview to *Avvenire*, daily newspaper of the Italian Bishops Conference, March 16, 2016, quoted in www.lifesitenews.com, March 16, 2016.

10. Gilles Routhier, Cardinal Leger biography, Dictionary of Canadian Biography, www.biographi.ca/en/bio/leger_paul_emile_22E.html

11. http://www.inquisition.ca/en/serm/winnipeg.htm

12. Msgr Vincent Foy, *Is there a Positive Side to the Winnipeg Statement*, available at www.msgrfoy.com; Msgr Vincent Foy, "Fifty reasons why the Winnipeg Statement should be recalled", *Catholic Insight*, October 2003; Msgr Vincent Foy, "Recovering Humanae Vitae in Canada", *Catholic Insight*, October 2010.

Chapter 2

1. http://www.biographi.ca/en/bio/trudeau_pierre_elliott_22E.html Dictionary of Canadian Biography. Trudeau's background is based on this.

2. Trudeau, Pierre, *Memoirs*, (McClelland & Stewart: Toronto, 1993) p. 40.

3. Mills, Dr. Allen, *Citizen Trudeau, 1944-1965: An Intellectual Biography* , (Oxford University Press, 2016)

4. For archival issues of *Esprit*, see http://www.esprit.presse.fr/tous-les-numeros.

5. Trudeau, *Memoirs,* p.47

6. Plamondon, Bob, *The Truth About Trudeau*, (Great River Media: Ottawa, 2013) , p.229; he quotes Trudeau *Memoirs,* and David Somerville, *Trudeau Revealed by His Actions and Words*, (BMG Publishing: Richmond Hill, 1978)

7. Plamondon, *op cit,* p.230 quoting Max Nemni and Monique Nemni, *Young Trudeau 1919-1944*, p.154

8. Mills, *Citizen Trudeau*, p.366; Dan Di Rocco, in his review of the manuscript stated that "Trudeau was way ahead of his time. In Canada today we have legislation being passed that effectively will make it a crime to deny that there are not more genders than just male and female. Where does this come from? Many sources, but certainly this type of thinking cited here is quite congruent with the laws and attitudes being expressed today."

9. Trudeau, *Memoirs*, p.64

10. Much of this section is based on de Valk, *Morality*, pp.27-34; for details on Section 150, see http://laws-lois.justice.gc.ca/eng/acts/C-46/page-33.html#h-56

11. *Ibid,* p.29

12. De Valk, *Morality,* pp.29-30 quoting Contraception, Divorce, Abortion: Three Statements by Canadian Catholic Conference, Ottawa, 1968, pp.64 and Proceedings, Birth Control, Oct 11, 1966 p/466ff.

13. De Valk, *Morality*, pp.31-2 quoting "Bishops express views on divorce", *Prairie Messenger,* April 12, 1967.

14. *Ibid*, p.34

15. Peter C. Newman, *Ottawa Journal,* April 26, 1967

16. Trudeau, *Memoirs*, pp.82-3.

17. De Valk, *Morality*, p.36 quoting *The Globe and Mail*, April 7, 1967

18. *Ibid*, p.37 quoting "Stand on Abortion Clarified", *Prairie Messenger,* April 26, 1967.

19. *Ibid,* pp.27-8

20. *Ibid,* pp.44-6 covers this section

21. House of Commons, the Standing Committee on Health and Welfare, Minutes of Proceedings, 2 volumes, henceforth Proceedings ...Abortion, Oct 9, 1967, quoted in De Valk, Morality, p.48.

22. De Valk, *Morality,* p.50-51 quoting Proceedings ... Abortion, Appendix F, p168 fn.; *The Globe and Mail*, November 8, 1967.

23. *Ibid*, p.55 quoting "Report to the House", Proceedings – Abortion, Dec 19,

1967, pp.14-3, 14-4.

24. *Ibid*, p.56 quoting *The Globe and Mail*, Dec 20, 1967; "A bold New Program that Touches us All" and *The Globe and Mail*, Dec 23, 1967.

25. *Ibid*, p.57 quoting *The Globe and Mail*, Dec 22, 1967.

26. "Trudeau's Real Legacy: Abortion, Divorce, Tyranny", Oct 03-2000, LifeSite Special Report, http://www.lifesite.net/ldn/2000/oct/001003a. html ; Steve Jalsevac, "The Real Pierre Trudeau – Father of Canada's Permissive Society", LifeSiteNews.com, Oct 3, 2000

27. *The Secular State*, 1985, by Fr. Alphonse de Valk; this is noted in "Trudeau's Real Legacy: Abortion, Divorce, Tyranny", Oct 03,2000, LifeSite Special Report, http://www.lifesite.net/ldn/2000/oct/001003a.html

28. De Valk, *Morality*, pp.59-63; on p.62 he references *The Catholic Register*, Jan 6, 1968

29. *Ibid*, Appendix V, pp.162-165.

30. *Ibid*, p.60 quoting *Relations*, Feb 1968, p.52.

31. *Ibid*, pp.79-80

32. Dehler, David, *The New Canadian Ethic – Kill our Unborn Canadians*, (Ottawa: Kanda, 1980), p.23.

33. De Valk, *Morality*, pp.84, 108,116-119, 126, 129-30; Fr de Valk references Hansard January 23, 1969, February 13, 1969, pp.5493-4, April 17, 1969, pp.7637-9, April 28, 1969, p.8056

34. Dehler, *The New Canadian Ethic*, pp.66-7.

35. De Valk, Morality, p.165.

36. Dehler, *The New Canadian Ethic*, p.42; the quote on Wolfenden is on p.80; the quote on bedrooms is on p.81.

Chapter 3

1. Robert Fulford, *National Post*, September 29, 1999

2. Trudeau, *Memoirs*, p.95

3. Plamondon, *Truth* , p.303; see also Steve Jalsevac, "The Real Pierre Trudeau – Father of Canada's Permissive Society", LifeSiteNews.com, Oct 3, 2000

4. Plamondon, *Truth*, pp.301-3

5. Trudeau, *Memoirs*, p.115.

6. Plamondon, *Truth*, p.89 his quote comes from Trudeau, *Federalism*, pp.103-123

7. Trudeau, *Memoirs*, p.164

8. Plamondon, *Truth*, p. 238, quoting Nemni, *Young Trudeau*, p.292

9. Plamondon, *Truth*, p.91 quoting Max Nemni and Monique Nemni, *Trudeau Transformed: the Shaping of a Statesman, 1944-1965*, McClelland & Stewart: Toronto, 2007), p.410

10. Paul Litt, *Elusive Destiny: the political vocation of John Napier Turner*, (UBC Press: Vancouver, 2011), p.231, quoted in Plamondon, *Truth*, p.93

11. Minutes of proceedings and Evidence of the Special Joint Committee of the Senate and the House of Commons on the Constitution of Canada, Third Session, Twenty-Eight Parliament, 1970-71, Issue No.62, Thursday,

April 1, 1971, Toronto, pp. 62:38 – 62:41

12. Minutes of proceedings and Evidence of the Special Joint Committee of the Senate and the House of Commons on the Constitution of Canada, Third Session, Twenty-Eight Parliament, 1970-71, Issue No.62, Thursday, April 1, 1971, Toronto, pp. 62:42 – 62:43

13. Minutes of proceedings and Evidence of the Special Joint Committee of the Senate and the House of Commons on the Constitution of Canada, Third Session, Twenty-Eight Parliament, 1970-71, Issue No.62, Thursday, April 1, 1971, Toronto, p. 62:45

14. Minutes of proceedings and Evidence of the Special Joint Committee of the Senate and the House of Commons on the Constitution of Canada, Third Session, Twenty-Eight Parliament, 1970-71, Issue No.62, Thursday, April 1, 1971, Toronto, pp. 62:44 - 62:45

15. Minutes of proceedings and Evidence of the Special Joint Committee of the Senate and the House of Commons on the Constitution of Canada, Third Session, Twenty-Eight Parliament, 1970-71, Issue No.62, Thursday, April 1, 1971, Toronto, pp. 62:46-62:47

16. Clement, Dr. Dominique, Will Silver, Dr. Daniel Trottier, *The Evolution of Human Rights in Canada,* Canadian Human Rights Commission, (Minister of Public Works and Government Services, 2012), available at http://www.chrc-ccdp.gc.ca/sites/default/files/ehrc_edpc-eng.pdf

17. Claude Belanger, The Pepin-Robarts Commission in http://faculty.marianopolis.edu/c.belanger/quebechistory/federal/pepin.htm

18. Bastien, Frederic, *The Battle of London: Trudeau, Thatcher and the Fight for Canada's Constitution,* (Toronto: Dundurn, 2013), p.43; John English, *Just Watch Me,* pp.383-4 states "Trudeau acknowledged the report in the House of Commons but refused to endorse it. Pepin told his wife that a prime ministerial aide had confided to him that, when Trudeau was handed the report, he tossed it immediately in the waste basket without reading it."

19. Interview with Jim Hughes, January 13, 2013; the details on Campaign Life were provided by Mary Ellen Douglas in her review of this manuscript, June 2016, and by Gwen Landolt in her review of November 2016.

20. Brief contained in the following document: *The Catholic Women's League of Canada , "Canada and its Future – A New Constitution",* a Brief to The Prime Minister of Canada The Rt. Hon Pierre Elliott Trudeau and the Minister of Justice The Hon Jean Chrétien

21. Nathanson, Bernard, *Aborting America,* (Doubleday & Company, Inc. 1959), p. 193.

22. Nathanson, Bernard, *The Hand of God: A Journey from Death to Life by the Abortion Doctor Who Changed His Mind,* (Washington, D.C.: Regnery Publishing, April 1, 1996)

23. Manitoba Pro-Life News magazine, in November 1980 quoting *Montreal Catholic Times,* April 1980

24. Plamondon, op cit, pp.155-6

25. *Ibid,* p.157; Dan di Rocco, a member of Campaign Life and a reviewer of

this book, wrote, on June 2016: "This was one of the most subtle and truly pernicious ways to undermine traditional morality and rights of people. It became part of school curriculum and further promoted his own wacky ideas about what Canada was about, what citizenship meant, and the whole rights revolution. We have seen where this hocus pocus has led. It really was a masterful plan by Trudeau and company, under the guise of modernization and other reforms.

26. Plamondon, *op cit*, pp.212-4

27. De Valk, *Morality*, pp. 129-156; see also Fr. de Valk, "The Abortion issue in Contemporary Canadian History: the Unfinished Debate", *CCHA*, *Study Sessions*, 41(1974), pp.81-99 available online at http://www.umanitoba.ca/colleges/st_pauls/ccha/Back%20Issues/CCHA1974/DeValk.html

28. Brief contained in the following document: *The Catholic Women's League of Canada*, "*Canada and its Future – A New Constitution*", a Brief to The Prime Minister of Canada The Rt. Hon Pierre Elliott Trudeau and the Minister of Justice The Hon Jean Chrétien

29. Gwen Landolt, paper Dec 6, 2016; Coalition for Life, National Newsletter, Number 6, June 1975; www.abortionlaws.ca/1970s.html; www.weneedalaw.ca/rsources/abortion-timeline notes that the petition "was soundly ignored by the government led by Mr. Trudeau"; www.pregnancy.mb.ca/quote-4.htm.

30. Dehler, *The New Canadian Ethic*, pp.6-14; Campaign Life Newsletter entitled "Recent Pro-Life Developments in Canada; no date but their brief had not yet been presented; speech by John Stephens, QC, nd but believed to be 1982

Chapter 4

1. The Canadian Bar Association's Report on the Constitution, Gerard V. La Forest, *Towards a New Canada*, (Montreal: Pierre Desmarais Inc., 1978) p.10

2. Canadian Unity Information Office, 111E (6-78) 20 Notes on Canadian Federalism, 1978

3. http://www.biographi.ca/en/bio.php?id_nbr=8418, Dictionary of Canadian Biography; John English, *Just Watch Me*, p.385 notes that at the Toronto rally Trudeau stated "he would give the provinces one last chance. If they failed to grasp it, the Federal government would act unilaterally to bring the Constitution home."

4. Plamondon, *op cit*, p.100

5. https://en.wikipedia.org/ wiki/ Liberal_Party_of_Canada_candidates, _1979_Canadian_federal_election -; www.cyclopaedia.info/ wiki/ Progressive-Conservative-Party-of-Canada-candidates, -1979-Canadian-federal-election

6. Bastien, *Battle*, p.51.

7. Renaissance, the Voice of Canada's Moral Majority, Manifesto and Petition to Candidates of all political parties in the forthcoming election of February 18, 1980

8. https://en.wikipedia.org/wiki/File:Canada_1980_Federal_Election.svg
9. Trudeau, *Memoirs*, p.284
10. Plamondon, *op cit*, p.105
11. Bastien, *Battle*, pp.73-4, 80.
12. Trudeau *Memoirs*, pp.308-310
13. Letter, Toth to CCCB, June 1980
14. Trudeau *Memoirs*, pp.308-310
15. Letter, Toth to CCCB, June 1980
16. *The Christian Enquirer*, March 1981
17. August 1980, Beverley Baines, Assistant Professor, Faculty of Law, Queen's University prepared a paper for the Advisory Council on the Status of Women, August 1980, entitled "Women, Human Rights and the Constitution".
18. Plamondon, op cit, p.206
19. http://www.biographi.ca/en/bio.php?id_nbr=8418, Dictionary of Canadian Biography
20. *Liberal Outlook*, # 9, Fall 1980, published by the Liberal Party of Canada (Ontario)
21. *Ibid.*
22. House of Commons debates, for Tuesday, October 7, 1980, Lorne Nystrom.
23. October 2, 1980, The Prime Minister Pierre Trudeau, Release on proposed Constitution
24. 25005-2-10-80, the Prime Minister presented the Proposed Resolution for a Joint Address to her Majesty the Queen respecting the Constitution of Canada.
25. Trudeau, *Memoirs,* p.312
26. CTV Question Period, Bruce Phillips, Pamela Wallin, Charles Lynch, Peter Lloyd, Oct 16, 1981
27. The *Toronto Star* , October 29, 1980; Chaviva Hosek, "How Women fought for Equality", Canadian Forum, May 1983
28. *The Globe and Mail*, November 16, 1980
29. Brief presented by the Coalition for the Protection of Human Life to the Commission, Dec 10, 1980
30. Letter March 19, 1981 Joseph Magnet to Fr. Dennis Murphy
31. Ontario Conference of Catholic Bishops, Brief to the Special Joint Committee on the Constitution of Canada, Dec 22, 1980
32. Letter, JohnMunro to Kathleen Toth, President of Campaign Life Nov 3, 1980
33. Letter Beatty to Toth, Nov 21, 1980
34. Brief to the Special Joint Committee on the Constitution of Canada; Constitution of Canada, 8-1-1981, 34:116-34:130; see also Minutes of Proceedings of the Special Joint Committee, v.3, January 8, 1981, p.34: 117-130, speech by Gwen Landolt
35. James Richardson, national Chairman, Canadians for one Canada, presented his brief to the Special Joint Committee on Dec 16, 1980

36. House of Commons Debates, Thursday October 23, 1980, p.4029

37. *National Catholic Reporter*, Jan 26, 1981; Fr. Alphonse de Valk, "Charter Clearly denies Rights"; *The Globe and Mail*, Nov 14, 1980

38. *Toronto Star*, November 15, 1980

39. Leslie Plommer, "British role urged in BNA discussion", *The Globe and Mail*, Dec 4, 1980

40. Jan 19, 1981, Campaign Life, urgent newsletter, "The life of the unborn child, the charter of rights and abortion clinics"

41. The Right to Life Association of Toronto and Area, "Analysis of the Proposed Constitution and How it will Affect the Rights of the Unborn Child in Canada, nd

42. Letter, Landolt to *The Globe & Mail*, *Toronto Sun*, *Toronto Star*, January 12, 1981

43. Letter, Landolt to Chrétien, Jan 28, 1981; Dan di Rocco, member of Campaign Life and reviewer of this book, wrote in June 2016: "the effect of these protestations is that they signaled to the government and the abortionists exactly how to go about taking away rights from the unborn child and expanding the radical abortion claims of the left wing pro-aborts. The Liberal Party and Trudeau and Chrétien were all in cahoots on the matter. And strategies to adopt along the way. It was masterful on their part."

44. News Release, Gwen Landolt, legal counsel for the Right to Life Association of Toronto and Area, March 16, 1981; Fr de Valk calculated that some 500,000 had been killed by 1985. Interview June 20, 2016; there has been much comment on government obfuscation of numbers; for example, see the *National Post*, August 10, 2012 at http://www.imfcanada.org/archive/679/national-post-ontario-cuts-access-abortion-records-highly-sensitive; also http://www.realwomenofcanada.ca/lack-of-accurate-numbers-turns-canadas-abortion-argument-into-guesswork/ and http://www.realwomenofcanada.ca/good-news-on-the-abortion-front-reality-2/ which discuss the issue.

45. Plamondon, *op cit*, p.204.

Chapter 5

1. Bastien, *Battle*, pp.115-6.

2. Newsletter, October 1980, Right to Life Association of Toronto and Area

3. "More power for courts stiffly opposed by PEI", *The Globe & Mail*, Jan 13, 1981

4. Stan Darling, MP House of Commons debates, March 5, 1981

5. Senate debates, February 24, 1981

Chapter 6

1. Jim Hughes interview January 13, 2013

2. Letter Fr. A.J. Macdougall, SJ, the General Secretary of the OCCB in a letter, dated June 27, 1978, to Paul Formby, National Co-coordinator of Campaign Life; see also letter May 20, 1981 Jim Hughes, chairman of Campaign Life Toronto & Area, Paul Dodds, Chairman, Campaign Life

Ontario and Kathleen Toth, president, Campaign Life Canada to the Canadian Bishops

3. Letter, Fr. Patrick Kennedy, Assistant General Secretary of the CCCB to Toth, President Campaign Life, Dec 3, 1980

4. Jim Hughes interview, January 13, 2013.

5. Letter, Fr. Patrick Kennedy, Assistant General Secretary of the CCCB, to Kathleen Toth, Dec 18, 1980

6. Letter, Cardinal Carter to Jim Hughes, Jan 10, 1980; letter, Fr. Patrick Kennedy, Assistant General Secretary of the CCCB asked Kathleen Toth, Jan 20, 1981;

7. Letter, Appeal to all Canadian Bishops, Jan 27, 1981

8. Letter Landolt to Cardinal Carter, Feb 10, 1981; letter, Landolt to Taitinger, Feb 11, 1981; Landolt to MPs, Feb 11, 1981

9. Letter, Feb 13, 1981 Ursula Appolloni; John Stephens speech, n.d. (1982)

10. March 31, 1981, Memorandum, Ursula Appolloni to all Liberals as well as MPs MacEachen, Killens, Campbell, Dingwall, Tobin and others.

11. Garnet Bloomfield interview, November 1, 2012; Gwen Landolt, "The Immorality of the Law", November 3, 2001, paper presented to Alliance for life, Ontario provincial Conference 2001; Interview with former Liberal MP Garnet Bloomfield", The Interim, December, 2013

12. Letter, Msgr. Dennis Murphy to Kathleen Toth, April 6, 1981

13. Jim Hughes interview Jan 13, 2013

14. Turcotte, Family Survival Fund, to Canadian Bishops, April 17, 1981

15. Jan de Villiers letter to Landolt, A Final Warning, April 14, 1981

16. Campaign Life news release, April 29, 1981

17. Letter, March 26, 1981 Archbishop MacNeil to Trudeau; background paper on Bishops position March-April 1981

18. Letter, Douglas Roche, n.d., summarizing Bishops actions prior to the charter vote.

19. letter, May 26, 1981, Joseph N. MacNeil, president of the Canadian Conference of Catholic bishops to Trudeau

20. Toronto Star June 5, 1981

21. Letter, Trudeau to Archbishop MacNeil, July 6, 1981

22. Letter, Pierre Fortin, executive assistant to Jean Chrétien to Kathleen Toth, Aug 5, 1981

23. Francis Alban & Christopher A Ferrara , Fatima Priest, (Good Counsel Publications, Pound Ridge, NY, 2013), p.40; they noted that Cardinal Carter, shortly after approving the charter, was granted the highest honour in the land, the Order of Canada, by Trudeau, Sauve, Turner, Chrétien et al. It can be truly said that the government of Canada never forgets a favour.

24. Campaign Life News, Alberta Newsletter – April 1981

25. Campaign Life Special Bulletin, May 2, 1981

26. Jim Hughes interview, January 13, 2013, Gwen Landolt comments.

27. Letter John Stephens to Ursula Appolloni, May 13, 1981

28. Letter May 20, 1981 Jim Hughes, chairman of Campaign Life Toronto & Area, Paul Dodds, Chairman, Campaign Life Ontario and Kathleen Toth, president, Campaign Life Canada to the Canadian Bishops
29. Letter, Formby to Campaign Life members, May 25, 1981
30. Letter, Shea to MacNeil, Sept 20, 1981
31. Letter, Murphy CCCB to Shea, Sept 24, 1981
32. *Toronto Star*, April 10, 1981
33. Jim Hughes interview, January 13, 2013
34. Background paper on position of CCCB, March-April 1981; *The Globe and Mail*, April 3, 1981; *Toronto Star* April 3, 1981;
35. *The Globe and Mail*, Sept 8, 2007, George Hutchison, "How Bill Davis Came to see the Light".
36. Paikin, Steve, *Bill Davis Nation Builder, and not so Bland After All*, (Dundurn Publishers: Toronto, 2016), pp.326-343.
37. Letter, Paul Formby to Canadian Catholic bishops, Nov 11, 1981

Chapter 7

1. Turcotte, Family Survival Fund, to Canadian Bishops, April 17, 1981
2. Research Office of the Official Opposition, March 12, 1981
3. Letter, Roche to Landolt, Feb 20, 1981
4. Thomas Siddon, House of Commons debates, March 5, 1981
5. David Crombie, House of Commons Debates, November 27, 1981
6. House of Commons Debates, Pierre Trudeau, November 27, 1981; others like Ed Broadbent, supported Trudeau, see newsletter, Ed Broadbent , Dec 9, 1981
7. Letter, Jean Morse-Chevrier to Paul Formby, Dec 10, 1981
8. *Toronto Star*, November 28, 1981; in Letter, Landolt to John Rist, Dec 14, 1981, it is noted the vote was 64 to 129
9. Letter, Jake Epp, MP to C. W. Fleming, Nov 26, 1981
10. Letter, Peter Elzinga to Toth, Dec 10, 1981
11. Campaign Life, Life March newsletter, Oct 15, 1981
12. Letter, David Kilgour to Kathleen Toth, Dec 9, 1981

Chapter 8

1. Letter, Gwen Landolt, CL to Jake Epp, Jan 21, 1981
2. *The Spectator*, Jan 22, 1981
3. Letter, Serge Joyal to Gwen Landolt, Feb 9, 1981
4. Feb 12, 1981, Robert Bockstael, MP, asked Mildred Morton, Research Branch, Law and Government Division
5. Letter, David Dehler to James MacGrath, copying Trudeau, Clark, Chrétien and many others, Feb 12, 1981
6. Hamilton Right to Life, Urgent Statement of the Proposed Constitution, February 1981; The Right to Life Association of Toronto and Area issued a similar statement.

7. John V Stephens to the Members of the House of Commons Pro-Life Committee, Feb 27, 1981; he followed this up with a letter to the members of the House of Commons, March 3, 1981

8. Letter, Dinsdale to Chrétien, March 5, 1981

9. Right to Life Association of Toronto and Area, Constitution Update, March 9, 1981

10. Chrétien to Landolt, March 24, 1981; John Stephens speech, nd, (1982)

11. Gwen Landolt paper on omission of God, March 27, 1981

12. Letter from Campaign Life executive to Pope John Paul II, May 12, 1981

13. Gwen Landolt, "The Charter of Rights and Traditional Values", April 20, 1981

14. Letter, Toth CL to MPs, Jan 30, 1981

15. *Toronto Star*, Nov 26, 1981; Letter, Jean Morse-Chevrier to Paul Formby, Dec 10, 1981; *Toronto Star*, Jan 11, 1982 Jean Morse-Chevrier letter

16. CTV Question Period, Bruce Phillips, Pamela Wallin, Charles Lynch, Peter Lloyd, Oct 16, 1981

17. Campaign Life newsletter – the ERA – Beware, Oct 26, 1981

18. Campaign Life newsletter, Oct 22, 1981

19. Letter, Paul Formby, Campaign Life to bishops of Canada, Nov 12, 1981

20. Renaissance Petition, Ken Campbell to Edward Schreyer, Oct 10, 1981

21. Ken Campbell Evangelistic Association, Inc, Encounter vol.X, n0.1 Winter 1981, insert dated February 1981

22. *Toronto Sun*, March 15, 1981, includes photo of Ken Campbell

23. *The Christian Inquirer*, March 1981

Chapter 9

1. Trudeau, *Memoirs*, pp.314-5;

2. Bastien, Frédéric, *La Bataille de Londres. Dessous, secrets et coulisses du rapatriement constitutionnel*, Éditions du Boréal (April 2013) English Translation by Jacob Homel, 2014 *The Battle of London: Trudeau, Thatcher, and the Fight for Canada's Constitution*, Dundurn Toronto Pages 336-338

3. In a speech in 1991 opening the Bora Laskin library at the University of Toronto, Trudeau said the minority should have ruled, *The Globe and Mail*, March 23, 1991

4. *Toronto Star*, Sept 29, 1981

5. *Toronto Sun*, Sept 30, 1981

6. Letter, Landolt to Biggs-Davidson, Aug 24, 1981

7. Letter, Fr. Lalonde, OMI to Landolt, Aug 31, 1981

8. Letter, Landolt to John Finnis, Oct 15, 1981

9. Letter, Kay Cleverley to Landolt, Oct 15, 1981

10. Letter, Marcus Fox and 18 others *London Times*, Oct 29, 1981

11. Trudeau, *Memoirs*, pp.317-9; Plamondon, *op cit*, pp.112-3; *Le Devoir*, Jan 12, 1982, letter by Michel Roy

12. *The Globe and Mail*, Nov 6, 1981; *Toronto Star*, Nov 6 & 7, 1981

13. Plamondon, *op cit*, pp.112-4
14. *National Post*, September 12, 2012
15. Notice Constitutional Agreement, 9 provinces and Canada sign, Nov 5, 1981
16. Trudeau, *Memoirs*, op cit, pp.323-4; Plamondon, *op cit*, p.113
17. Plamondon, *op cit*, pp.112-3
18. Plamondon, *op cit*, p.114
19. Notice Constitutional Agreement, 9 provinces and Canada sign, Nov 5, 1981
20. Bastien, *Battle*, p.320.
21. House of Commons Debates, 32nd Parliament, 1st session: Vol.12, p.13042 November 20, 1981 speech by Jean Chrétien
22. House of Commons Debates, 32nd Parliament, 1st session: Vol.12, p.13048 November 20, 1981, speech by Joe Clark
23. Ibid. p.13217, November 24, 1981, speech by Ray Hnatyshyn.
24. Gwen Landolt, "*The Immorality of the Law*", November 3, 2001, presented to Alliance for Life, Ontario Provincial Conference 2001
25. Letter, Toth to MPs, Nov 19, 1981; Don Mazankowski to Toth, Nov 23, 1981; Judith Larocque to Toth, Nov 26, 1981; Albert Chambers to Toth, 8 Dec 1981; Edward Gorecki to Toth, Nov 24, 1981
26. Letter, Landolt to Roche, Nov 19, 1981; Landolt to John Finnis, Jan 12, 1982 expresses possible arguments on provincial rights not being respected
27. Telepost Cardinal Carter to Trudeau, Nov 25, 1981; *Toronto Star*, Nov 26, 1981; *Catholic Register*, Dec 5, 1981
28. Letter, Toth to MPs, Nov 30, 1981;
29. Letter Landolt to John Rist, Dec 14, 1981; the latter noted that since his stroke the Cardinal had become very concerned about the rights of the unborn.
30. House of Commons Debates, November 26, 1981
31. John Stephens speech (n.d.) 1982
32. House of Commons Statement from Garnet M. Bloomfield, November 20, 1981
33. S. M. Hudecki, press release Abortion Issue and Constitution, noted Dec 3, 1981
34. *The Globe and Mail*, Dec 3, 1981; Jean Morse-Chevrier to Paul Formby, Dec 10, 1981
35. Letter, Toth to The Senate of Canada, Dec 4, 1981
36. *Toronto Star*, Dec 5, 1981; *Toronto Sun*, Dec 8, 1981; Jean Morse-Chevrier to Paul Formby, Dec 10, 1981
37. Plamondon, *op cit*, p.115, 216.
38. Gwen Landolt, "*The Immorality of the Law*", November 3, 2001, presented to Alliance for Life, Ontario Provincial Conference 2001
39. Campaign Life newsletter, Nov 10, 1981

Chapter 11

1. *Ottawa Citizen* March 1st, 1988; *Toronto Star* March 1st, 1988
2. Senate Legal and Constitutional Affairs Committee on October 29, 1990, brief by Kim Campbell.
3. *The Interim,* April 5, 1991 quoting from the Ottawa Citizen

Conclusion

1. *Toronto Star,* Saturday, October 11, 1980
2. Manitoba Pro-Life News magazine, in November 1980; Campaign Life Newsletter entitled "Recent Pro-Life Developments in Canada; no date but their brief had not yet been presented; letter Kathleen Toth, president of Campaign Life, October 23, 1980
3. The Catholic Women's League of Canada, *"Canada and its Future – A New Constitution",* a Brief to The Prime Minister of Canada The Right Hon Pierre Elliott Trudeau and the Minister of justice The Hon Jean Chrétien; letter, National President CWL to Presidents, Dec 1, 1980
4. Manitoba Pro-Life News magazine, in November 1980
5. *Ibid.*
6. Letter, Jim Hughes quoted by Dan di Rocco to Redmond, August 17, 2016

Bibliography

Primary Sources

Gwen Landolt, correspondence archives.
Jim Hughes, interview January 13, 2013
Garnet Bloomfield, interview November 1, 2012

Campaign Life
Archives, including newsletters, press releases and correspondence

Canadian Bar Association
Proceedings Canadian Bar Association, 1966

Canadian Conference of Catholic Bishops
Contraception, Divorce, Abortion: Three Statements by Canadian Catholic Conference, Ottawa, 1968;
Proceedings, Birth Control, Oct 11, 1966.

Catholic Women's League
"*Canada and its Future – A New Constitution*", a Brief to the Prime Minister of Canada the Rt. Hon Pierre Elliott Trudeau and the Minister of Justice the Hon Jean Chrétien
Ontario Conference of Catholic Bishops, Brief to the Special Joint Committee on the Constitution of Canada", Dec 22, 1980

Coalition for Life
National Newsletters

Government of Canada
Minutes of Proceedings and Evidence of the Special Joint Committee of the Senate and the House of Commons on the Constitution of Canada
Canadian Unity Information Office, 111E (6-78) 20 Notes on Canadian Federalism, 1978
Government of Canada, House of Commons
Hansard, various years
October 2, 1980, The Prime Minister Pierre Trudeau, Release on proposed Constitution
25005-2-10-80, the Prime Minister presented the Proposed Resolution for a Joint Address to her Majesty the Queen respecting the Constitution of Canada
Notice Constitutional Agreement, 9 provinces and Canada sign, Nov 5, 1981
http://parl.canadiana.ca/view/oop.debates_HOC3201
Dates included in volumes 1 to 12:
Vol. 1 April 14, 1980 to May 15, 1980
Vol. 2 May 16 to June 19
Vol. 3 June 20 to Oct 8
Vol. 4 Oct 9 to Nov 13
Vol. 5 Nov 14 to Dec 17
Vol. 6 Dec 18, 1980 to Feb 9, 1981

Vol. 7 Feb 10, 1981 to Mar 12, 1981
Vol. 8 Mar 13 to Apr 21
Vol. 9 Apr 22 to June 12
Vol. 10 June 15 to July 17
Vol. 11 Oct 14 to Nov 18
Vol. 12 Nov 19 to Dec 14, 1981

Ontario Conference of Catholic Bishops
Brief to the Special Joint Committee on the Constitution of Canada, Dec 22, 1980

Ontario Medical Association,
Report of the Special Committee on Therapeutic Abortions and Sterilizations, May 1965

Renaissance, the Voice of Canada's Moral Majority, Manifesto and Petition to Candidates of all political parties in the forthcoming election of February 18, 1980

Publications

Alban, Francis & Christopher A. Ferrara, *Fatima Priest*, (Good Counsel Publications: Pound Ridge, NY, 2013)

Anonymous, *The Vatican II Revolution 1962-1965*, available at http://www.mostholyfamilymonastery.com/8_ VaticanII.pdf

Anonymous, *The Heresies of Vatican II; Decrees of the Ecumenical Councils*, Vol. 2, http://www.mostholyfamilymonastery.com/8_ VaticanII.pdf

Anonymous, *Decrees of the Ecumenical Councils*, Vol. 2

Anonymous, *the Papal Encyclicals*, Vol. 2 (1878-1903)

Anonymous, *Decrees of the Ecumenical Councils*, Vol. 2

Anonymous, *Renaissance, the Voice of Canada's Moral Majority*, Manifesto and Petition to Candidates of all political parties in the forthcoming election of February 18, 1980

Anonymous, "Trudeau's Real Legacy: Abortion, Divorce, Tyranny", Oct 03-2000, LifeSite Special Report, http://www.lifesite.net/ldn/2000/oct/001003a.html

Bastien, Frederic, *The Battle of London: Trudeau, Thatcher and the Fight for Canada's Constitution,* (Toronto: Dundurn, 2013)

Baines, Beverley, Paper for the Advisory Council on the Status of Women, August 1980, entitled "Women, Human Rights and the Constitution".

Belanger, Claude, *The Pepin-Robarts Commission* in http://faculty.marianopolis.edu/c.belanger/quebechistory/federal/pepin.htm;

Benedict XVI, *Principles of Catholic Theology*, San Francisco, CA: Ignatius Press, 1982

Clarkson, Stephen & Christina McCall, *Trudeau and our Times, Volume 1: The Magnificent Obsession*, (Toronto: McClelland & Stewart, 1991)

Clement, Dr. Dominique, Will Silver, Dr. Daniel Trottier, *The Evolution of Human Rights in Canada,* Canadian Human Rights Commission, (Minister of

Public Works and Government Services, 2012), available at http://www.chrc-ccdp.gc.ca/sites/default/files/ehrc_edpc-eng.pdf

Dehler, David, *the New Canadian Ethic – Kill our Unborn Canadians*, (Ottawa: Kanda, 1980)

Denzinger, *the Sources of Catholic Dogma*, (B. Herder Book. Co., Thirtieth Edition, 1957)

De Valk, Fr Alphonse, CSB, *Morality and Law in Canadian Politics – The Abortion Controversy*, (Montreal: Palm Publishers, 1974)

De Valk, Alphonse, CSB, "The Abortion issue in Contemporary Canadian History: the Unfinished Debate", *CCHA, Study Sessions*, 41(1974), pp.81-99 available online at http://www.umanitoba.ca/colleges/st_pauls/ccha/Back%20Issues/CCHA1974/DeValk.html

De Valk, Fr. Alphonse, CSB, "Pluralism and Secularism in Canadian Law and Society", *CCHA, Study Sessions*, 50 (1983), pp.631-54.

De Valk, Fr. Alphonse, CSB, *The Secular State, 1985*, this is noted in "Trudeau's Real Legacy: Abortion, Divorce, Tyranny", Oct 03-2000, LifeSite Special Report, http://www.lifesite.net/ldn/2000/oct/001003a.html

De Valk, Fr. Alphonse, "Charter clearly denies Rights"; *The Globe and Mail*, Nov 14, 1980

Dimond, Brother Michael, *Michael Davies: Defender of the Faith or Faithless Heretic,* http://www.mostholyfamilymonastery

English, John, *Just Watch Me*, (Vintage Canada, 2010)

Foy, Monsignor Vincent, *Is there a Positive Side to the Winnipeg Statement*, available at www.msgrfoy.com

Foy, Monsignor Vincent, "Fifty reasons why the Winnipeg Statement should be recalled", *Catholic Insight*, October 2003;

Foy, Monsignor Vincent, "Recovering Humanae Vitae in Canada", *Catholic Insight*, October 2010.

Goodall, Rev. Ray, "Is Abortion ever Right", *Chatelaine*, March 1963

Hosek, Chaviva, "How Women fought for Equality", *Canadian Forum*, May 1983

Hutchison, George, "How Bill Davis Came to see the Light", *The Globe & Mail*, Sept 8, 2007.

Jalsevac, Steve, "The Real Pierre Trudeau – Father of Canada's Permissive Society", www.LifeSiteNews.com, Oct 3, 2000

La Forest, Gerard, The Canadian Bar Association's Report on the Constitution, *Towards a New Canada*, (Montreal: Pierre Desmarais Inc, 1978)

Litt, Paul, *Elusive Destiny: the political vocation of John Napier Turner*, (UBC Press: Vancouver, 2011)

Landolt, Gwen, "The Immorality of the Law", November 3, 2001, paper presented to Alliance for Life, Ontario Provincial Conference 2001

Mills, Allen, *Citizen Trudeau, 1944-1965: An Intellectual Biography*, (London: Oxford University Press, 2016)

Nathanson, Bernard, *Aborting America,* (Doubleday & Company, Inc. 1959)

Nathanson, Bernard, *The Hand of God: A Journey from Death to Life by the*

Abortion Doctor Who Changed His Mind, (Washington, D.C.: Regnery Publishing, April 1, 1996)

Nemni, Max and Monique Nemni, *Trudeau Transformed: the Shaping of a Statesman, 1944-1965,* McClelland & Stewart: Toronto, 2007)

Nemni, Max and Monique Nemni, *Young Trudeau 1919-1944: Son of Quebec, Father of Canada*, (Douglas Gibson Books: Montreal, 2006), p.154

Paikin, Steve, *Bill Davis – Nation Builder and not so Bland after All*, (Toronto: Dundurn Press, 2016)

Plamondon, Bob, *the Truth About Trudeau*, (Great River Media: Ottawa, 2013)

Plommer, Leslie, "British role urged in BNA discussion", *The Globe and Mail*, Dec 4, 1980

Ratzinger, Cardinal Joseph, *Principles of Catholic Theology*, (Ignatius: San Francisco, 1982).

Routhier, Gilles, *Cardinal Leger biography*, Dictionary of Canadian Biography, www.biographi.ca/en/bio/leger_paul_emile_22E.html

Somerville, David, *Trudeau Revealed by His Actions and Words*, (BMG Publishing: Richmond Hill, 1978)

Trudeau, Pierre, *Memoirs*, (McClelland & Stewart: Toronto, 1993)

Other Websites

http://www.biographi.ca/en/bio/trudeau_pierre_elliott_22E.html Dictionary of Canadian Biography.

https://en.wikipedia.org/ wiki/ Liberal_Party_of_Canada_candidates, _1979_ Canadian_federal_election -; www.cyclopaedia.info/ wiki/ Progressive-Conservative-Party-of-Canada-candidates, -1979-Canadian-federal-election

http://www.biographi.ca/en/bio.php?id_nbr=8418_; Dictionary of Canadian Biography

https://en.wikipedia.org/wiki/File:Canada_1980_Federal_Election.svg

Media

The Globe and Mail, Toronto Sun, Manitoba Pro-Life News Magazine, Campaign Life newsletters; *The Christian Enquirer; Catholic Register;*

Right to Life Association of Toronto and Area newsletters; Hamilton Right to Life newsletter; Encounter;

CTV Question Period, Bruce Phillips, Pamela Wallin, Charles Lynch, Peter Lloyd, Oct 16, 1981

Index

A

Abortion, ii, iii, v, 1-7, 12-3, 18-33, 40-51, , 53-4, 71-85, 88, 90, 94, 97, 100-118, 125-8, 130-46, 152, 158, 161-189, 191, 195

Abortion caravan, 45-7

Abortion committee, 18-9, 21-3, 27, 30, 32, 41, 45, 5050

Adams, Dr. Paul, 22

Ad Hoc Committee of Pro-Life Women, 141

Ad Hoc Women's Conference, 131

Advisory Council on the Status of Women, 49-50, 64, 76, 81, 134

Aitken, Dr. D. M., 6

Aitken, Jonathan, 153

Ajax Pro-life, 40-1

Alban, Francis, 112, 192

Alfrink, Cardinal Bernard Jan, 9

Alkenbrack, Mr. 30

Alliance for Life, 22, 44, 51-2, 98, 173, 179, 181-2, 192, 195

Allmand, Warren, 164

All Party Committee, 153

American Law Institute, 3

Amyotte, Earl, 43, 103, 134

Anderson, Doris, 3, 48-9, 78

Anglican Church, 5, 28

Anguish, Doug, 127, 150

Appolloni, Ursula, 52-3, 101-4, 115, 192-3

Association of Catholic Hospitals, 25, 27

Association of Doctors for the Repeal of the Abortion Law, 53, 170

Azzi, Stephen, 156

B

Badgley Committee, 53-4

Badgley, Dr. Robin F., 53

Baines, Beverley, 64, 190

Baker, George, 127

Barry, Dr. Michael, 74

Basford, Ron, 49

Bastien, Frederic, 43, 61, 87, 159, 168, 188-91, 194, 195

BC Catholic Lawyers Guild, 4

Bea, Cardinal Augustin, 9

Beatty, Perrin, 70, 74, 76, 190-1

Beaudoin, M. 30

Beetz, Justice, 170

Begin, Monique, 49

Belanger, Claude, 188

Nesbitt, Mr. 30

Neuhaus, Fr. Richard John, 184

New Democrat Party, 21, 29, 30, 51, 60, 65-6, 70, 74, 124, 130-1, 135, 150-1, 164, 178

Newfoundland, 27, 65, 69, 94, 149, 155-7

Newman, Peter, 20, 186

New Woman Centre, 49

Noble, Mr. 30

Norris, Peggy, 151

Notes on Canadian Federalism, 58

Notwithstanding Clause, 155-61

Nurses for Life, 41

Nuyens, Dr. Andreas J., 55

Nystrom, Lorne, 66, 70, 74-5, 150, 190

O

Official Languages Act, 62

Official Secrets Act, 64

Ogle, Fr. Bob, 127, 130, 135, 164

O'Keefe, Joseph, 22

Omnibus Bill, ii, v, 2, 23, 25-6, 28-9, 45, 50,117

Ontario Conference of Catholic Bishops, 73, 98, 118, 173, 190

Ontario Court of Appeal, 55, 135, 137, 150

Ontario Human Rights Commission, 50

Ontario Medical Association, 5-6, 185

Ontario Superior Court, 54

Ottawa Pro-life, 40, 164

P

Paikin, Steve, 119, 193

Paikin, Sydney, 5,

Paproski, Mr. 30

Parliamentary supremacy, 37, 42, 50, 57, 58, 61-2, 70, 72, 74-5, 77, 80-4, 87-95, 106, 108, 124, 126-8, 130, 133, 134-8, 140, 152, 159-60, 162, 177

Parti Quebecois, 42

Pearson, Lester, 17, 18, 20, 27

Peate, George, 48

Peckford, Brian, 65, 94, 155-7

Peddle, Mr. 30

Pell, Cardinal George, 184

Pelletier, Gerald, 16, 17

Pentecostal Assembles of Canada, 28, 100, 173

Peoples Church, 117

Pepin, Jean-Luc, 42

About the authors

C. Gwendolyn Landolt

C. Gwendolyn Landolt graduated from the Faculty of Law, University of British Columbia, Canada and was called to the British Columbia Bar.

She has had an extensive legal career in private practice, as a Crown prosecutor and as a lawyer with the federal government where she specialized in immigration and aboriginal affairs.

Mrs. Landolt has written extensively on Canadian constitutional issues, in particular the Canadian Charter of Rights and has participated in more than thirty cases, mostly before the Supreme Court of Canada.

Mrs. Landolt is the founder and first president of Right to Life in Toronto and the Greater Toronto Area. She is one of the founders of Campaign Life Canada where she served as legal counsel. She also served as legal counsel for Toronto Right to Life. She was founder of Canadian Advocates for Human life (Pro-Life lawyer association); and was a member of the executive of the National Alliance for Life for five years and was National President from 1975 to 1978.

Mrs. Landolt is one of the founders and is currently National Vice President of REAL Women of Canada, a national women's organization founded in 1983. The organization is committed to the protection of the traditional family and human life, both in Canada and internationally. REAL Women is an NGO in SPECIAL consultative status with the Economic and Social Council of the United Nations where she has participated on many conferences around the world.

Patrick Redmond

Patrick Redmond received a BA in African History from Loyola College, Montreal, then an MA in Swahili from Duquesne University in Pittsburgh, and a PhD in African History from the University of London, England.

Afterwards he taught history and archaeology at the University of the West Indies in Trinidad, WI, for a year, then at the Abdullahi Bayero Campus of the University of Zaria in Kano, Nigeria for three years.

In 1976, he returned to Canada and joined IBM, where he worked for 31 years.

He became involved in the pro-life movement, particularly with York South Right to Life, of which he was president for many years. He joined Campaign Life and other pro-life and family groups. He ran for the Family Coalition Party in two elections and one by-election, promoting pro-life and family causes.

He has published numerous articles, as well as the following books:

Irish Life in Rural Quebec - A History of Frampton, 1977
The Politics of Power in Songea Ngoni Society 1860-1962, 1985
From Adam and Eve to the Present - A Human Journey, 2012

72696479R00142

Made in the USA
Columbia, SC
25 June 2017